MOVE IT!

STUDENTS' BOOK

SPLIT EDITION

1B

CAROLYN BARRACLOUGH, KATHERINE STANNETT

SERIES CONSULTANT: CARA NORRIS-RAMIREZ

5 Out and About!

Grammar
Present continuous;
Present simple and
Present continuous

Vocabulary
Activities; Weather
and seasons

Speaking
Expressing surprise

Writing
A blog

Word list page 27
Workbook page 128

Vocabulary • Activities

1 Match the photos to these words. Then listen, check and repeat.

2.13

bowling
climbing
dancing
gymnastics
hiking
horseback riding
ice skating
kayaking
mountain biking
painting
playing an instrument
rollerblading
singing
surfing *1*

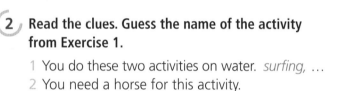

2 Read the clues. Guess the name of the activity from Exercise 1.

1 You do these two activities on water. *surfing, …*
2 You need a horse for this activity.
3 You need a bicycle for this activity.
4 You use a ball in this activity.
5 You walk a lot in this activity.
6 You make music in these two activities.

3 Listen. Copy and complete the activities Joe and
2.14 Lisa do at the Vacation Camp.

	morning	afternoon
Joe	*mountain biking*	
Lisa		

4 Write three sentences about activities you like
and don't like.

I like rollerblading, but I don't like kayaking.

**Brain Trainer
Activity 3**
Go to page 62

Reading

1 Read the text quickly. Match the photos (1–4) to the correct paragraphs (A–D).

2 Read the text and check your answer to Exercise 1.

3 Read the text again. Choose the correct options.

2.15
1 Ricardo *is* / *isn't* at college today.
2 The first thing Ricky does is *mountain biking* / *climbing*.
3 The reporter, Amanda, *likes* / *doesn't like* hiking up Corcovado Mountain.
4 Ricky and Amanda are on Copacabana beach in the *morning* / *afternoon*.
5 A lot of people in Brazil *like* / *don't like* surfing.
6 Ricky is very good at *swimming* / *surfing*.

4 Guess the job. Then listen to Ricky and check.

2.16

5 What about you? In pairs, ask and answer.
1 What sports/activities are popular in your country?
2 What sports do you like?
3 What activities do you usually do in your free time?

> What sports are popular in your country?

> A lot of people like rollerblading.

Guess the Job!

Reporter Amanda Moreno is spending the day with nineteen-year-old Ricardo Dos Santos. He's a college student from Brazil.

A It's 6 a.m., and I'm having breakfast with Ricardo—nickname Ricky—on Corcovado Mountain in Rio de Janeiro. It's December, so the weather is great at the moment. The students aren't studying—they're on vacation. Today I'm taking photos of Ricky for our **Guess the job!** competition.

B Ricky's first activity today is mountain biking. He isn't riding down the street—he's riding up the street. It isn't easy!

C It's 11 a.m. Now we're hiking up the mountain for Ricky's next activities. I'm not enjoying it, but Ricky likes walking and climbing. Now we're at the top. Ricky is rollerblading and skateboarding. He's having fun!

D Now it's 4 p.m. We aren't on the mountain; we're on Copacabana beach. Ricky is swimming and surfing. Surfing is a popular sport here, and Ricky is very good at it. But why is he doing all these activities? Can you guess the job?

Is Ricky …
a a professional sports player?
b a stuntman in a movie?
c a vacation camp counselor?
Email your answers to:
guessthejob@smart.com

Grammar • Present continuous

Affirmative	
I	'm (am) singing.
He/She/It	's (is) singing.
You/We/They	're (are) singing.
Negative	
I	'm (am) not singing.
He/She/It	isn't (is not) singing.
You/We/They	aren't (are not) singing.
Questions and short answers	
Am I singing?	Yes, I am. No, I'm not.
Is he/she/it singing?	Yes, he/she/it is. No, he/she/it isn't.
Are you/we/they singing?	Yes, you/we/they are. No, you/we/they aren't.

Grammar reference page 118

Watch Out!
run → running   write → writing
have → having

1 Study the grammar table. Choose the correct options to complete the rules.

1 The verb *to do* / *to be* goes before the main verb in the Present continuous.
2 We add *-ing* / *-es* to the end of the main verb.
3 The verb *to be* goes *before* / *after* the main verb in questions in the Present continuous.

2 Write the *-ing* forms of the verbs.

1 go *going*   3 do   5 swim   7 play
2 watch   4 have   6 walk   8 run

Pronunciation *-ing* endings

3a Listen to the verbs and the *-ing* endings
2.17 from Exercise 2.

b What sound does the *i* make?
2.17 Say *-ing* aloud.

c Listen again and repeat.
2.17

4 Make sentences.

1 Juan (not get up / sleep).
  Juan isn't getting up. He's sleeping.
2 Enrique and Erica (not ice skate / bowl).
3 Mr. Chapman (not surf / sing).
4 Adriana and I (not study / dance).
5 I (not skateboard / paint my room).
6 Ms. Green (not swim / run).

5 **Complete the text with the verbs. Use the Present**
2.18 **continuous. Listen and check.**

The dance act you ¹ *are watching* (watch) now is the Hot Street Crew! Look at this! Kayla ² .... (not dance); she ³ .... (do) gymnastics here! Now Leroy and Des ⁴ .... (jump)! They ⁵ .... (have) fun! In the studio, the audience ⁶ .... (not sit) down. Everyone is standing and clapping. What a great dance!

6 Look at the picture and answer the questions.

It's 9 p.m. in Puebla, Mexico.
1 Is the Morales family sitting in the living room?
  Yes, it is.
2 Is Elena watching TV?
3 Is her mom writing a letter?
4 Is the dog having dinner?

7 Make questions. Ask and answer for Elena.

1 your dog / sleep?
2 your parents / read?
3 you / sit / next to your mom?
4 you and your parents / eat / pizza?

8 What about you? Imagine it's 6 p.m. on Saturday. What are you doing now?

I'm listening to my favorite band on my MP3 player.

Vocabulary • Weather and seasons

1 Match the pictures to these words. Then listen,
2.19 check and repeat.

autumn/fall	cloudy	cold	foggy	hot
raining *1*	snowing	spring	summer	sunny
warm	windy	winter		

Word list page 27
Workbook page 128

2 Look at the picture. Complete the sentences with
2.20 the weather words from Exercise 1. Then listen,
check and repeat.

What's the weather like today?
Let's look at the weather in the US. In Texas,
the weather is ¹ *hot* right now.
In California, it's a nice ² .... day. But it's ³ ....
in Alabama. It's ⁴ .... there, too.
Montana is very ⁵ .... , and it's ⁶ .... as well.
In Florida, they have nice ⁷ .... weather,
but it's ⁸ .... , too.
And in Michigan, the weather isn't cold,
but it's ⁹ .... .

3 Listen. Choose the correct weather.
2.21
1 **a** It's raining. **b** It's cold. **c** It's foggy.
2 **a** It's sunny. **b** It's snowing. **c** It's cloudy.
3 **a** It's windy. **b** It's cloudy. **c** It's sunny.
4 **a** It's cold. **b** It's warm. **c** It's hot.

4 Look at the map in Exercise 2. In pairs,
ask and answer.

Is it foggy
in Montana?

No, it isn't.

**Brain Trainer
Activity 4**
Go to page 62

Chatroom Expressing surprise

Speaking and Listening

1 Look at the photos. Which of these things can you see?

1 a dog   4 a rat
2 a farm   5 a river
3 an otter   6 a bridge

2 Listen and read the conversation.
2.22 Answer the questions.

1 Where are the children?
They are at Willow End.
2 What does Monica often do in the summer?
3 Is Nick filming Julia and Monica?
4 What animals are in the water?
5 What are these animals doing?
6 What does Julia tell Nick to do?

3 Act out the conversation in groups of three.

Monica	We're here! This is Willow End. It's my favorite place. It's nice in the summer—I often swim in the river here.
Julia	But not today! Brrr! The water's very cold.
Nick	Wow! This is an amazing place!
Monica	Look at the bridge.
Julia	Great! I love it!
Monica	Hey! Are you filming us with your cell phone, Nick?
Nick	No. I'm looking at that animal in the water.
Julia	Yuck! Is it a rat?
Monica	No, it's an otter. I sometimes see them here.
Nick	Really? There aren't many otters. They're very rare. Look! Two otters! They're swimming.
Julia	How amazing! Take a photo, Nick.

Say it in your language ...
We're here!
Yuck!

4 Look back at the conversation. Match an expression to each object.

1 Wow!
2 Great!
3 How amazing!

a Willow End
b the otters
c the bridge

5 Read the phrases for expressing surprise.

Something nice surprises you	You are surprised by some information	You are surprised by an event
Wow! Great! How amazing!	Really?	Look! Hey!

6 Listen to the conversation. Act out the conversation in pairs.
2.23

Stella Hi, Steve. It's me, Stella. Guess what I'm doing!
Steve I don't know. ¹ Are you shopping at the mall?
Stella No. I'm ² having coffee in the Rain Forest Café.
Steve Really?
Stella And ³ Brad Pitt is standing near me. I'm taking a photo.
Steve Wow! How amazing!

7 Work in pairs. Replace the words in purple in Exercise 6 with these words. Act out the conversation.

> Are you going to the movies?

> No. I'm bowling with my friends.

1 eating at a pizza place / sitting on a bus / going to a baseball game

2 watching a baseball game / waiting for a movie premiere / going to a concert

3 actor / singer / athlete

8 Act out the conversation again with your own words and ideas.

Grammar • Present simple and Present continuous

Present simple	Present continuous
I often swim here.	They're swimming.
I sometimes see them.	He's looking at the animals now.

Watch Out!
always, usually, often, sometimes, hardly ever, never → every day / week / month
happening now, at the moment

Grammar reference page 118

1 Study the grammar table. Match the tenses to the actions.

1 Present simple
2 Present continuous

a action happening now
b routine

2 Do we use the Present simple or the Present continuous with these words?

1 now *Present continuous*
2 always
3 every week
4 today
5 usually
6 never
7 at the moment

3 Are these sentences in the Present simple (Ps) or Present continuous (Pc)?

1 They're playing soccer at the moment. *Pc*
2 My grandma comes for dinner every Sunday.
3 Do you usually get up at 6 a.m.?
4 Jim isn't watching TV now.
5 He is studying today.
6 We get up late on Saturdays.

4 Choose the correct options.

1 Harry and Lucy *go / are going* on a school trip.
2 I often *do / am doing* my homework in the living room.
3 He *doesn't go / isn't going* ice skating every day.
4 *Do they climb / Are they climbing* at the moment?
5 Jenny *gets up / is getting up* late on Saturdays.
6 The dog *doesn't sleep / isn't sleeping* now.

Reading

1 Look quickly at the texts. What kind of texts do you think they are?

  1 articles   2 emails   3 poems

The Fog

I like the fog,
It's soft and cool,
It hides everything,
On the way to school.

I can't see a house,
I can't see a tree,
Because the fog
Is playing with me.

The sun comes out,
The fog goes away,
But it will be back
Another day.

Anonymous

Weather

Weather is hot,
Weather is cold,
Weather is changing
As the weeks unfold.

Skies are cloudy,
Skies are fair,
Skies are changing
In the air.

It is raining,
It is snowing,
It is windy
With breezes blowing.

Days are foggy,
Days are clear,
Weather is changing
Throughout the year!

Meish Goldish

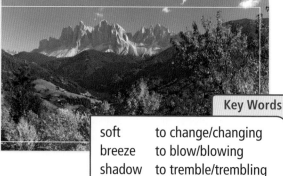

Autumn wind
The mountain's shadow
is trembling

Kobayashi Issa

Key Words	
soft	to change/changing
breeze	to blow/blowing
shadow	to tremble/trembling

2 Read and check your answer to Exercise 1.

3 Read this definition of a haiku. Which poem is a haiku?

A haiku is a very short Japanese poem. A haiku usually talks about one of the four seasons.

4 Read the poems again. Answer the questions.
2.24
  1 Does "The Fog" poet like fog? *Yes, he does.*
  2 Is the "Weather" poem talking about weather at one time of year?
  3 Which season is the haiku about?
  4 Which poem has four stanzas?
  5 Which poem doesn't use rhyme?
  6 How many weather words can you find in all the poems?

Listening

1 Listen and match the people (1–3) to the season
2.25 they are talking about.

  1 Blake   a spring
  2 Yoko   b summer
  3 Paolo   c fall

2 Listen again. Are the statements true (T)
2.25 or false (F)?

  1 Blake is from Canada.
  2 Blake likes the color of autumn flowers.
  3 Yoko is American.
  4 Cherry blossoms are pink and white.
  5 Paolo likes summer.
  6 Summer in Argentina is in July.

Writing • A blog

1 Read the Writing File.

> **Writing File**   Word order
>
> The subject of a sentence comes before
> the verb in English.
> *I get up at 6 a.m.*
> *Sam and Anna are having breakfast.*

2 Read Julio's blog. Find the verbs that follow
these subjects.

1 I   2 he/Erik   3 we

Monday Morning

I usually get up later, but today I'm getting up
at 6:30 a.m. because I'm in Norway!

We're on a school exchange trip to Tromsø,
a city in the Arctic Circle. It's really cold here!
It's snowing now, and it's foggy, too. In winter
there are usually only a couple of hours of light
in the day.

Erik is my exchange buddy. He lives here,
and he loves winter sports. He often goes
kayaking and ice skating. Do you know that
Tromsø is Norway's candidate for the 2018
Winter Olympics?

It's 7 a.m. now, and Erik is waiting for me
with snowshoes. We use them to go
to school—it's cool!

Julio

3 Put the words in the correct order
to make sentences.

1 writing / her blog / is / Layla
   Layla is writing her blog.
2 go to school / We / at eight thirty
3 The dog / swimming / in the river / is
4 like / rollerblading / They
5 Nat and Mia / are / in the mountains / hiking

4 Read the blog again. Answer the questions.

1 Why is Julio in Norway?
   Because he is on a school exchange trip.
2 What is the weather like in Tromsø?
3 Is it light all day in Tromsø in winter?
4 What activities does Erik like?
5 What is Erik doing now?

5 Imagine you are on an exchange trip. Answer
the questions about your trip.

1 What time do you usually get up?
2 Are you doing things at different times today?
3 Where are you?
4 What is the weather like in this place?
5 What is the weather like at home?
6 Who is your exchange buddy?
7 What activities does he/she like?

6 Write a short blog about your exchange trip. Use
"My blog" and your answers from Exercise 5.

> **My blog**
>
> **Paragraph 1**   introducing a topic
> *I usually … , but today I … .*
>
> **Paragraph 2**   talking about a place
> *It's … in … .* (place)
>
> **Paragraph 3**   talking about a person
> (name) *is … .*
> *He/She lives / likes / often goes … .*

Remember!
● Check word order for subjects and verbs.
● Use the vocabulary in this unit.
● Check your grammar, spelling
  and punctuation.

Refresh Your Memory!

Grammar • Review

1 Complete the postcard with the verbs in the Present continuous.

Hi Tania,

We ¹ *'re enjoying* (enjoy) our family vacation in Tampa. I ² .... (sit) by the swimming pool with my little brother, Jack. I ³ .... (watch) him because my parents ⁴ .... (make) dinner.

Jack ⁵ .... (not swim) at the moment. He ⁶ .... (play) with some cats. The cats ⁷ .... (run) away from my brother—they ⁸ .... (not have) fun!

See you soon,

Nicole

Tania Bexon
34 Hancock St
Dover, NH 03820

2 Make questions with the Present continuous.

1 you / sit / in a classroom?
   Are you sitting in a classroom?
2 your teacher / talk / to the class?
3 you / watch / TV?
4 you and your friend / talk?
5 all the students / listen / to the teacher?
6 your friend / write / in his/her notebook?

3 Answer the questions in Exercise 2.

1 *Yes, I am.*

4 Put the verbs in the Present simple or the Present continuous.

1 Georgia (brush) her teeth every morning.
   Georgia brushes her teeth every morning.
2 We (have) our breakfast now.
3 It (not rain) at the moment.
4 He often (hike) in the spring.
5 They (rollerblade) in the park now.
6 She never (watch) TV after 10 p.m.
7 He (study) every day.
8 I (visit) my grandma today.

Vocabulary • Review

5 Find the one that doesn't fit.

1 **a** kayaking
  b *horseback riding*
  c surfing
2 **a** ice skating
  b singing
  c dancing
3 **a** climbing
  b hiking
  c playing an instrument
4 **a** rollerblading
  b bowling
  c painting
5 **a** singing
  b horseback riding
  c hiking

6 Complete the sentences with a weather word.

1 It isn't sunny today. It's r*aining.*
2 It's warm today, but it's c _ _ _ _ _, too.
3 It's very cold today, and it's s _ _ _ _ _ _ now.
4 The weather is w _ _ _ _ and cold today.
5 This morning it's very gray and f _ _ _ _ outside.

Speaking • Review

7 Choose the correct option to complete each
2.26 conversation. Then listen and check.

1
Girl *Hey! / Wow!* What are you doing?
Boy I'm taking a photo of you! Smile!

2
Girl Guess what! I have tickets for the Kings of Leon concert tonight!
Boy *Look! / Really?*

3
Boy Jennifer Lopez is sitting near me.
Girl *How amazing! / Hey!*

Dictation

8 Listen and write in your notebook.
2.27

✓ **My assessment profile:** page 142

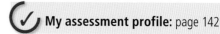

Why Is the Sky Blue?

This experiment shows us why the sky is blue.

You need …

- a flashlight
- a 1-liter plastic bottle
- some milk
- some water

1 Put 750 ml of water into the bottle.

2 Put the flashlight under the bottle and turn it on. Look down on it from above. What color is the light?

3 Add one teaspoon of milk to the water and mix it together. Shine the flashlight again and look down on the bottle. Now the light in the middle of the bottle is orange, and the light at the sides of the bottle is blue.

Why does this happen?

The light from the flashlight has a lot of different colors. When it passes through the milk and water mixture, it breaks up into different-colored light waves. The blue light wave is short. The orange light wave is long. So the blue light wave is at the side of the bottle, and the orange light wave is at the top of the bottle.

In the same way, light from the sun breaks up into different colors when it comes into our atmosphere. In the day, we see the short blue light waves. At sunset and at sunrise, we see the long red and orange light waves.

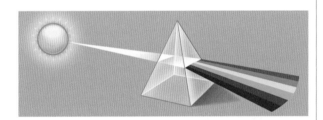

Reading

1 Read the text quickly. Match 1–2 to a–b.

1 Blue light waves are …   a long.
2 Orange light waves are …   b short.

2 Read the text again. Answer the questions.

2.28

1 What color is the light in the middle of the bottle? *orange*
2 What color is the light at the sides of the bottle?
3 What happens when the light passes through the water and milk mixture?
4 What happens when light from the sun comes into our atmosphere?

My Science File

3 Find out about rainbows. Find out …

- when rainbows happen.
- why we see rainbows.

4 In pairs, create an experiment to make a rainbow. Use some of these things:

- a flashlight
- a glass
- a bottle of water
- a sheet of paper
- a mirror
- a CD or DVD
- a window

5 Write your instructions for the experiment in your notebook.

6 Delicious!

Grammar
Countable and uncountable nouns;
Many/Much/A lot of;
Comparatives

Vocabulary
Food and drinks;
Adjectives

Speaking
Ordering food

Writing
Instructions

Word list page 27
Workbook page 129

Vocabulary • Food and drinks

1 Match the pictures (1–16) to these words. Then listen, check and repeat.

2.29

banana	bread	broccoli	cheese	chicken	eggs
ham	juice	pasta	rice	salmon	sausage
shrimp	tea	tomatoes	tuna	water	yogurt *1*

2 Copy and complete the table with food from Exercise 1.

Carbohydrates	Fish
bread, ...	*tuna, ...*
Fruits and Vegetables	**Dairy**
banana, ...	*cheese, ...*
Meat	**Drinks**
sausage, ...	*water, ...*

3 In pairs, ask and answer.

1 What do you usually have for breakfast/ lunch/dinner?
2 What's your favorite food?
3 What's your favorite drink?

> What do you usually have for breakfast?

> I usually have bread and cheese.

**Brain Trainer
Activity 3**
Go to page 63

Reading

1 **Look at the photos. Write *Juanita*, *Caitlin* or *Chuck*.**

1 This person's refrigerator has some fruits in it.
2 This person's refrigerator has 24 eggs in it.
3 This person's refrigerator has 10 carrots in it.

2 **Read and check your answers to Exercise 1.**

3 **Read the article again. Are the statements true (T) or false (F)?**

2.30

1 Juanita doesn't have any fish in her fridge. *F*
2 Juanita likes rice salad.
3 Caitlin likes meat.
4 Caitlin's family doesn't drink much water.
5 There is a lot of sausage in Chuck's fridge.
6 Chuck doesn't like yogurt.

4 **What about you? In pairs, ask and answer.**

1 What's in your fridge at home?
2 Are you a vegetarian?
3 Are you a good cook?
4 What food don't you like?

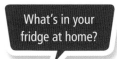

What's in your fridge at home?

I think we have some vegetables, cheese, ...

Look!
This Is Our Refrigerator!

Juanita

I live in El Calafate, a small town in Patagonia. Today we're preparing a barbecue, so we have a lot of chicken, sausage and salmon in our fridge. There's a rice salad with shrimp and tuna—it's delicious! We also have twenty-four eggs because my mom loves making cakes.

Caitlin

My family is from Scotland, and we're vegetarians, so we don't have any meat in our fridge. We usually have a lot of vegetables, and today we have some broccoli, ten carrots and a lot of tomatoes. We don't have any milk, and we don't have much juice, but that's OK because we all drink a lot of water.

Chuck

We're from Wisconsin. I have a big family and a very big fridge! Today we have some ham, a lot of bread and sausage. We don't have many eggs, but there's a lot of yogurt because we all love yogurt. We also have a lot of fruit because I often make smoothies for breakfast.

Grammar

• Countable and uncountable nouns

Countable nouns		Uncountable nouns
Singular	**Plural**	
a banana	some bananas	some bread
an apple	some apples	some rice
an egg	some eggs	some pasta

1 Study the grammar table. Choose the correct options to complete the rule.

> We use *much* / *many* with countable nouns and *much* / *many* with uncountable nouns.

2 Are these words countable or uncountable?

1 chicken *uncountable*
2 broccoli
3 vegetable
4 water
5 tomato

6 sausage
7 banana
8 salmon
9 tuna
10 yogurt

Pronunciation Word stress

3a Listen to the words in Exercise 2.
2.31 Where is the stress?

*chi**cken***

b Listen again. Copy and put the words
2.31 under the correct heading.

chicken	to**ma**to

c Listen again and repeat.
2.31

• Many/Much/A lot of

How many?	How much?
How many eggs do you have?	How much bread do you have?
We don't have any eggs.	We don't have any bread.
We don't have many eggs.	We don't have much bread.
We have some/four eggs.	We have some bread.
We have a lot of eggs.	We have a lot of bread.

Grammar reference page 120

4 Look at the picture. Choose the correct options.

1 How *much* / *many* pasta is on the table?
2 How *much* / *many* eggs are on the table?
3 How *much* / *many* bread is on the table?
4 How *much* / *many* cheese is on the table?
5 How *much* / *many* tomatoes are on the table?

5 Answer the questions in Exercise 4.
Use *not much/many* or *a lot of*.

1 *There is a lot of pasta.*

6 Complete the conversation with these words.

Not much   much   many   ~~some~~   a lot of

Chen What's in your lunch box, Billy?
Billy I have ¹*some* ham sandwiches.
Chen How ² .... sandwiches do you have?
Billy Four.
Chen That's ³ .... sandwiches! And how
⁴ .... water do you have?
Billy ⁵ .... . My water bottle is very small.

7 What about you? **What's in your favorite sandwich? In pairs, ask and answer.**

> What do you have in your sandwich?

> I have a lot of chicken and some tomatoes.

Vocabulary • Adjectives

1 Look at the pictures and choose the correct options to complete
2.32 the sentences. Then listen, check and repeat.

clean	cold	delicious	dirty	disgusting	horrible
hot	large	noisy	quiet	small	~~wonderful~~

Word list page 27
Workbook page 129

1 Fernando's is a *wonderful* / *horrible* restaurant!
2 The coffee is *hot* / *cold*.
3 The food is *disgusting* / *delicious*!
4 We have *small* / *large* tables.
5 The music is *quiet* / *noisy*.
6 The kitchen is very *clean* / *dirty*.

7 Fernando's is a *wonderful* / *horrible* restaurant!
8 The coffee is *hot* / *cold*.
9 The food is *disgusting* / *delicious*!
10 We have *small* / *large* tables.
11 The music is *quiet* / *noisy*.
12 The kitchen is very *clean* / *dirty*.

2 Say the opposites.

1 quiet *noisy*
2 small
3 clean
4 hot
5 delicious
6 horrible

3 Choose the correct options.

1 Don't eat this food! It's *clean* /
   delicious / *disgusting*.
2 I can't hear the radio. It's very
   small / *cold* / *quiet*.
3 I don't want this tea. It's *large* /
   noisy / *cold*.
4 There are 2,000 students in
   this school. It's a *quiet* / *large* /
   delicious school.
5 I like this book. It's *horrible* /
   wonderful / *quiet*.
6 Don't sit there. The table is
   noisy / *dirty* / *wonderful*.

4 Complete the text with these
2.33 words. Then listen and check.

clean	delicious	large
quiet	~~small~~	wonderful

I love visiting my aunt. She
lives in a ¹ *small* house in the
country with only two rooms,
but the yard is ² ....—it's almost
30 meters long! It's always
³ .... at my aunt's house because
there aren't any cars or people
near her. My aunt hates dirt, so
her house is always very ⁴ .... .
My favorite time of day at my
aunt's house is dessert. My aunt
is a ⁵ .... cook, and she makes
⁶ .... cakes. I love eating them!

Brain Trainer
Activity 4
Go to page 63

Chatroom Ordering food

Speaking and Listening

1 Look at the photo. Answer the question.

1 Where are Monica, Julia, Nick and Leo?

2 Listen and read the conversation.
2.34 Answer the questions.

1 Why are the children at the restaurant?
   It's Nick's birthday.
2 Do they sit at the small table
   or the large table?
3 What does Julia order?
4 Who orders the pasta with chicken?
5 Who orders some garlic bread?
6 Who doesn't want a drink?
7 Does Monica like her pizza?

3 Act out the conversation in groups of five.

Julia	Hi, everyone! Happy birthday, Nick! Is this table OK?
Nick	It's very small. That table's better. It's larger.
Monica	Yes, but it's much noisier. Let's stay here.
Julia	OK. Here's the menu.
Waiter	Are you ready to order?
Julia	Yes. I'd like the ham and cheese pizza, please.
Monica	Me too!
Nick	I'll have the pasta with chicken, please. And some garlic bread. Yum!
Leo	Spaghetti with tomato sauce for me, please.
Waiter	And would you like anything to drink?
Monica	No, I'm OK, thanks.
Nick	Can we have some water, please?
Waiter	Yes, of course.
	***
Waiter	How is your food?
Monica	It's delicious, thanks.

Say it in your language …
Yum!
Yes, of course.

4 Look back at the conversation. What questions does the waiter ask? How do the children reply?

Waiter … *Are you ready to order?*

Children …

5 Read the phrases for ordering food in a restaurant.

Waiter	Customer
Are you ready to order? Would you like anything to drink? Yes, of course. How is your food?	I'd like the ham and cheese pizza, please. I'll have the pasta with chicken, please. Spaghetti with tomato sauce for me, please. No, I'm OK, thanks. Can we have some water, please? It's delicious, thanks.

6 Listen to the conversation. Act out the conversation in groups of four.

2.35

Waiter Are you ready to order?
Nick Yes. I'll have the ¹ cheese sandwich, please.
Monica I'd like the ² salmon with broccoli, please.
Julia I'll have the ³ tuna salad, please.
Waiter Would you like anything to drink?
Nick No, I'm OK, thanks.
Monica Me too!
Julia Can I have a glass of ⁴ orange juice, please?
Waiter Yes, of course.

7 Work in groups of four. Replace the words in purple in Exercise 6. Use these words and/or your own ideas. Act out the conversations.

 Are you ready to order?

 Yes. I'll have … .

1 ham sandwich / chicken sandwich / egg sandwich

2 sausage with carrots / tuna with tomatoes / pasta with shrimp

3 egg salad / ham salad / tuna salad

4 apple juice / water

Grammar • Comparatives

Short adjectives	
small	smaller
clean	cleaner
hot	hotter
Short adjectives ending in -e	
large	larger
Adjectives ending in -y	
dirty	dirtier
Long adjectives	
wonderful	more wonderful
Irregular adjectives	
bad	worse
good	better

Watch Out!
Her school is smaller than your school.
The pasta is more delicious than the pizza.

Grammar reference page 120

1 Study the grammar table. Complete the rules.

To make the comparative form, we add ¹…. to the end of a short adjective, and use the word ²…. in front of a long adjective.

2 Complete the sentences with the comparative adjectives.

1 My house is *colder* (cold) than your house.
2 This table is …. (noisy) than that table.
3 The chicken is …. (delicious) than the fish.
4 The poster is …. (cheap) than the DVD.
5 My watch is …. (new) than your watch.
6 Harry's camera is …. (expensive) than Sam's camera.

3 Work in pairs. Find five differences between you and your partner. Use these ideas.

1 old / young
2 long / short hair
3 large / small family
4 light / dark eyes
5 big backpack / small backpack

Reading

 1 Look at the photos. What are the places?

    a vacation camps
    b restaurants
    c hotels

Three Unusual ...

Every week we find three unusual places around the world. This week we're looking at amazing restaurants from three different countries.

1 Ithaa: The Undersea Restaurant

You can watch the fish and listen to the ocean in this restaurant. It's in the Maldives, and it's five meters below sea level. There is space for fourteen people in the restaurant. The food is expensive—dinner for two people is $150—but the view is wonderful.

2 The Treehouse Restaurant

Do you like being outside? Do you like looking at the trees and the sky? This restaurant is ten meters above the ground in a treehouse in a forest in New Zealand. You can have lunch or dinner, look at the trees and listen to the birds. Bring a sweater because it's cold here in the evenings.

3 Dinner in the Sky

The home of this restaurant is Belgium, but it can be in New York, London, Paris ... or in your hometown! It travels around the world on a big trailer. Do you want a view of a city or of the ocean? You can choose with "Dinner in the Sky." There is one large table with 22 chairs, and it is 50 meters above the ground! Don't look down!

Key Words		
unusual	below	space
outside	sweater	trailer

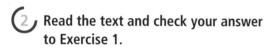 **2** Read the text and check your answer to Exercise 1.

 3 Read the text again. Answer the questions.

2.36

    1 Is Ithaa a cheap restaurant?
    No, it's an expensive restaurant.
    2 How many people can eat at Ithaa?
    3 Why do you need warm clothes for the Treehouse Restaurant?
    4 What animals can you listen to at the Treehouse Restaurant?
    5 How many people can eat at Dinner in the Sky?
    6 What's special about Dinner in the Sky?

Listening

 1 Match the national dishes (1–3) to the countries (a–c).

    1 empanada   **a** England
    2 moussaka   **b** Chile
    3 fish and chips   **c** Greece

2 Listen and check your answers to Exercise 1.

2.37

3 Listen again. Are the statements true (T)
2.37 or false (F)?

    1 Diego is from Greece.
    2 An empanada has meat or vegetables inside.
    3 There is fish and cheese in moussaka.
    4 A lot of people in England like fish and chips.

Writing • Instructions

1 Read the Writing File.

> **Writing File**   Sequence words
>
> First, open the bag.
> Then take out the chips.
> Finally, eat the chips.

2 Read the recipe. Find the sequence words *first*, *then* and *finally*.

 Chop!
 Add!
 Pour!

Banana and Raspberry Yogurt Smoothie

 Blend!

Ingredients
- 1 banana
- 10–12 raspberries
- 5 tablespoons of raspberry yogurt
- 3 tablespoons of milk

First, chop the banana. Put the banana into a blender. Then add the raspberries, the yogurt and the milk. Blend for thirty seconds. Finally, pour the mixture into a glass and drink it! You can add sugar, but it's better without sugar.

You can also make frozen smoothies with this recipe. First, pour the drink into small paper cups. Then put a stick into each cup and put the cups in the freezer. Finally, wait two hours and then take a cup out of the freezer. Enjoy your frozen yogurt smoothie!

 Smoothie

3 Put these sentences into the correct order. Rewrite them using *first*, *then* and *finally*.

How to make a cup of tea:
a add hot water.
b drink your tea.
c put the teabag into the cup.

4 Read the recipe again. Answer the questions.

1 How many bananas do you need? *one*
2 How much yogurt do you need?
3 Is the recipe better with some sugar?
4 Where do you put the paper cups?

5 Create your own milkshake recipe. Choose two or three ingredients from the list below.

ice cream
banana
raspberry
strawberry
mango
pineapple
cocoa

6 Write your recipe. Use "My milkshake" and your ingredients from Exercise 5.

> **My milkshake**
>
> .... and .... Milkshake
>
> Ingredients
> - *250 ml of milk*
> - *1 / 2 / 3 …*
> - *2 / 3 tablespoons of …*
>
> First, … . / Then … . / Finally, … .
> You can also make … .
> Enjoy your … .

Remember!
- Use sequence words (*first, then, finally*).
- Use the vocabulary in this unit.
- Check your grammar, spelling and punctuation.

Refresh Your Memory!

Grammar • Review

1 Are these words countable (C) or uncountable (U)?

banana C	broccoli	cheese	egg
ham	pasta	rice	sausage
shrimp	tomatoes	water	yogurt

2 Choose the correct options to complete the conversation.

Joe How *much / many* chicken do we have in the fridge?

Freda Not *much / many*.

Joe Oh, OK. What about eggs, and bread?

Freda We have *much / a lot of* eggs, but we don't have *much / many* bread.

Joe How *much / many* sausage do we have?

Freda We have half a kilo of sausage, but we don't have *any / no* ham.

Joe How *much / many* cheese do we have?

Freda We have *a lot of / much* cheese.

3 Make the comparative form of these adjectives.

1 delicious *more delicious*
2 large
3 dirty
4 small
5 cold
6 noisy
7 wonderful
8 clean

4 Make sentences with comparative adjectives.

1 Lucy's cell phone / small / Sally's cell phone
Lucy's cell phone is smaller than Sally's cell phone.
2 My bike / large / your scooter
3 The summer in California / hot / in Rhode Island
4 The Italian restaurant / good / the Chinese restaurant
5 My bedroom / clean / your bedroom
6 Your dog / noisy / my dog
7 Towns / quiet / cities
8 The pizza / delicious / the pasta

Vocabulary • Review

5 Complete the food words.

1 c h _e e s e_
2 t _ _ a _ _ _ s
3 b r _ _ _ _ _ i
4 j _ i _ _
5 _ r _ _ d

6 Complete the sentences with these words.

| clean | ~~delicious~~ | disgusting | large |
| quiet | small | wonderful | |

1 This egg sandwich is *delicious*, but it's very .... . I want another sandwich now!
2 You must have .... hands when you cook food.
3 My MP3 player's very .... ! I can't hear the music.
4 This yogurt is old. It's .... .
5 I love this movie. It's .... !
6 My cousin lives in a very .... house. It has six bedrooms and four bathrooms.

Speaking • Review

7 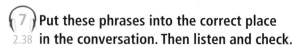 Put these phrases into the correct place in the conversation. Then listen and check.
2.38

| I'll have | It's delicious | ~~Are you ready to order?~~ |
| I'm OK | Would you like | |

Waiter ¹ *Are you ready to order?*
Greg Yes. I'd like the pasta with tomatoes, please.
Bea ² .... the chicken with broccoli, please.
Waiter ³ .... anything to drink?
Greg Yes, please. Can I have a glass of water?
Bea ⁴ .... , thanks.
Waiter How is your food?
Greg ⁵ .... , thank you.

Dictation

8 Listen and write in your notebook.
2.39

My assessment profile: page 143

Amy Singh's Profile

 Age
22

Home country
United States

City
New York City

Reading

1 **Read about Amy and chocolate.**
2.40 **Answer the questions.**

1 Why does Amy visit the Botanical Garden in 2002?
She wants to see a cacao tree.
2 What does Maricel Presilla give Amy in 2002?
3 Where does Amy make chocolate?
4 How does Amy's chocolate taste?
5 When does Amy make a speech at the New York Chocolate Show?
6 What does Amy do in 2007?
7 What is Amy's message?

Amy and Chocolate

Early 2002

Amy Singh is nine years old. Her fourth-grade teacher asks students to do a project about anything they want to study, and Amy decides to make chocolate at home. She visits the New York City Botanical Garden to see her first cacao tree.

Late 2002

Amy contacts Maricel Presilla, an author of a book about chocolate. Maricel meets with Amy and gives her a bag of cacao beans. Different chocolate companies tell Amy that you can only make chocolate in a factory. Amy creates machines from household objects to make chocolate in her kitchen. Maricel and other experts taste Amy's chocolate and say it's delicious!

2003

It's 2003, and Amy is 10 years old. She is invited to the New York Chocolate Show, where she gives a presentation about making chocolate at home.

2007

Amy is 15 years old. She learns about a serious problem in the chocolate industry: child labor. She makes a video about children working on cacao plantations. Her video is posted on the website of the International Labor Rights Fund.

May 2013

Amy is 21 and is invited to Prague, Czech Republic, to give a talk about her chocolate story. Amy's message is "Pursue your curiosity." And when there are problems, find your "little child's voice" and "let it inspire you."

Class discussion

• Imagine you can do a school project about anything you want, just like Amy. What is your project about? Why?
• Can you cook something? What?
• Why do you think Amy is successful? What can we learn from her story?

Grammar • Adverbs of frequency

1 Make sentences about the people in the table with these adverbs.

Ella always gets up before 7 a.m.

~~always~~	hardly ever	never
often	sometimes	usually

I get up before 7 a.m.	Ella	Mia + Jade	Tom	Zak	Ali	Jo
Number of days in a year	365	2	70	150	0	351

2 Make sentences.

1 go home / They / at three thirty / usually
   They usually go home at three thirty.
2 often / is / late / She
3 hardly / eat pasta / I / ever
4 We / watch a DVD / on Fridays / always
5 at the café / are / sometimes / They / at 4:15
6 He / uses / his MP3 player / never

• Present simple with *Wh* questions

3 Make *Wh* questions for the answers with these words.

How often	What	~~When~~	Where	Who	Why

1 you / play tennis / ?
   At 4:30.
   When do you play tennis?
2 your grandparents / live / ?
   In Florida.
3 your favorite movie / ?
   Star Wars.
4 he / have PE classes / ?
   Every day.
5 Tom Cruise / ?
   He's an actor.
6 you / like / science / ?
   Because it's interesting.

• Must/Mustn't

4 Make sentences with *must* or *mustn't*.

1 they / have / breakfast / before 8 a.m.
   They must have breakfast before 8 a.m.
2 he / not / watch / TV / today
3 I / do / my math homework
4 she / brush / her teeth / every day
5 we / not / be / late for class

• Present continuous

5 Complete the sentences with the Present continuous of the verbs.

1 He *'s singing* (sing) his favorite song.
2 We .... (have) lunch at the moment.
3 They .... (not clean up) their bedroom.
4 She .... (run) to school because she's late.
5 You .... (not watch) TV.

6 Make questions and answers with the Present continuous.

1 they / use / the computer / ?   ✗
   Are they using the computer? No, they aren't.
2 it / snow / at the moment / ?   ✓
3 I / do / the correct exercise / ?   ✓
4 you / bike / a long way / ?   ✗
5 they / swim / in the ocean / ?   ✗

• Present simple and Present continuous

7 Complete the conversation with the Present simple or Present continuous.

Luke Hi, Leah. What ¹ *are you doing* (you / do) at the train station?

Leah I ² .... (wait) for my friend Susan. She ³ .... (come) here for a week.

Luke That's great!

Leah Yes. I ⁴ .... (hardly ever / see) her because she ⁵ .... (swim) in competitions every weekend. What about you? Where ⁶ .... (you / go) now?

Luke To the beach.

Leah But it ⁷ .... (rain) today!

Luke I ⁸ .... (always / go) to the beach in the rain.

• Countable and uncountable nouns

8 **Are these words countable (C) or uncountable (U)?**

1 broccoli *U*   5 rice
2 egg   6 banana
3 sausage   7 tea
4 water   8 shrimp

9 **Choose the correct options.**

1 How *much* / *many* water do you have?
2 I'm eating *an* / *some* egg.
3 There isn't *much* / *many* juice in the fridge.
4 We have *a* / *some* bread.
5 Is there *much* / *many* shrimp in your pasta?

10 **Complete the conversation with these words.**

a	How many	How much	lot of
many	much	some (x2)	

A Let's make ¹ *a* pizza!
B ² .... cheese do we have?
A We have a ³ .... cheese. We have ⁴ .... broccoli, too. We have ⁵ .... ham, but we don't have very ⁶ .... .
B ⁷ .... tomatoes do we have? I love pizzas with tomato sauce!
A We don't have ⁸ .... tomatoes. Just a few.
B OK. Let's put them on the pizza, too. Yum!

• Comparatives

11 **Write the comparative form of the adjectives.**

1 cold *colder*   6 clean
2 large   7 dirty
3 disgusting   8 good
4 noisy   9 hot
5 bad   10 horrible

12 **Make sentences with the comparative form of the adjective.**

1 your bag: 2012 / her bag: 2013 (new)
  Her bag is newer than your bag.
2 my math grade: C / my history grade: A (good)
3 Chicago: 5°C / Miami: 25°C (cold)
4 his parents: 50 / your parents: 39 (old)
5 surfing: $15 / horseback riding: $30 (expensive)

Speaking • Expressing likes and dislikes

1 **Make sentences.**

1 I / like / play / tennis
  I like playing tennis.
2 I / love / swim
3 my sister / love / ice skate
4 I / not like / do / sports
5 I / hate / be / in the water

2 **Complete the conversation with the sentences from Exercise 1.**

A ¹*I love swimming.*
B I don't. ² .... .
A What's your favorite sport?
B Well, tennis is fun. ³ .... with my sister in the summer. ⁴ .... with her friends in the winter, but I never go with them. ⁵ .... when it's cold.

• Expressing surprise

3 **Complete the words.**

1 A I got an email from Tammi. She's in Istanbul.
  B W o w !
2 A I _ove tarantulas.
  B R _ _ _ _ y?
3 A I have a ticket to the Olympic Games.
  B H _ w a _ _ z _ _ _!
4 A L _ _ k! That movie with Ashton Kutcher is on TV.
  B Gr _ _ _! He's my favorite actor.

• Ordering food

4 **Put the conversation in the correct order.**

Customer 1	Can I have a glass of apple juice, please?	....
Waiter	Are you ready to order?	.1.
Customer 1	Yes. I'd like the salmon and rice, please. What about you, Phil?	....
Waiter	Would you like anything to drink?	....
Customer 2	Me too!	....
Customer 1	It's delicious, thank you.	....
Waiter	How is your food?	....
Customer 2	I'll have the tuna salad, please.	....

Review 2

Vocabulary • Unusual animals

1 Fill in the missing letters in the words.

1 p y g _m_ _y_ g _o_ a t
2 t _ r _ n t _ _ a
3 p y _ _ o n
4 p i _ _ n _ a
5 h i _ _ i n g c _ _ k r _ _ c h
6 p _ _ r _ t
7 s _ _ c k i _ s _ _ t
8 f _ _ g
9 g i _ _ t r _ _ b _ t
10 l _ z _ _ d

• Parts of the body

2 Complete the sentences with these words.

arms	beak	fingers	foot	~~head~~	legs
neck	paw	tail	toes	wings	

1 A python has a small *head* and a long body.
2 A dog has four .... , but a stick insect has six.
3 A cat has a long .... .
4 A giraffe has a long .... .
5 We have ten .... and ten .... .
6 At the end of my leg is my .... .
7 At the end of our .... , we have hands.
8 A .... is the name for a dog's foot.
9 A parrot flies with its .... and eats with its .... .

• Activities

3 Match the descriptions to these words.

climbing	hiking
~~kayaking~~	mountain biking
painting	playing an instrument
horseback riding	singing
~~surfing~~	

1 You do this on water. *kayaking, surfing*
2 You do this at a music lesson.
3 You do this in art class.
4 You can do this in a tree.
5 You ride something in this activity.
6 You walk a long way in this activity.

• Weather and seasons

4 Read Meiko's diary. Complete the words.

• January 10
I love [1] win _t e r_ in Japan. It's very [2] c _ _ _.
Today it's [3] s _ _ _ ing. I can go skiing soon!
• April 7
In [4] sp _ _ _ _ we admire the pink flowers on
the cherry trees. It's [5] w _ _ m outside.
• June 15
It's [6] r _ _ n _ _ _ today. I don't like this weather!
• July 27
[7] S _ _ _ er is here! It's very [8] h _ _ and [9] su _ _ _.
• October 2
It's [10] au _ _ _ _. There are red leaves on the
trees. It's [11] cl _ _ d _ and [12] f _ _ _ y today.
It's very [13] w _ _ d _, too.

• Food and drinks

5 Put the words in the correct categories.

bananas	bread	broccoli	~~cheese~~
chicken	eggs	ham	juice
pasta	rice	salmon	sausage
shrimp	tea	tomatoes	tuna
water	yogurt		

1 Dairy *cheese*   4 Fruits and Vegetables
2 Fish   5 Drinks
3 Meat   6 Carbohydrates

• Adjectives

6 Complete the sentences with these words.

clean	~~delicious~~	dirty	disgusting
large	noisy	quiet	wonderful

1 I love this food. It's *delicious*.
2 Giant rabbits are very .... .
3 Be .... . Your brother's sleeping.
4 I hate cockroaches. They're .... .
5 I'm nice and .... after my shower.
6 I'm always .... after playing soccer.
7 That parrot talks a lot. It's very .... .
8 We're having a .... vacation. I love it here!

Word list

Unit 4 • Animal Magic

Unusual animals

frog	/frɔg/
giant rabbit	/ˈdʒaɪənt ˈræbɪt/
hissing cockroach	/ˈhɪsɪŋ ˈkak-roʊtʃ/
lizard	/ˈlɪzɚd/
parrot	/ˈpærət/
piranha	/pɪˈranə/
pygmy goat	/ˈpɪgmi ˈgoʊt/
python	/ˈpaɪθan/
stick insect	/ˈstɪk ˈɪnsɛkt/
tarantula	/təˈræntʃələ/

Parts of the body

arm	/arm/
beak	/bik/
fin	/fɪn/
finger	/ˈfɪŋgɚ/
foot	/fʊt/
hand	/hænd/
head	/hɛd/
leg	/lɛg/
neck	/nɛk/
paw	/pɔ/
tail	/teɪl/
toe	/toʊ/
wing	/wɪŋ/

Unit 5 • Out and About!

Activities

bowling	/ˈboʊlɪŋ/
climbing	/ˈklaɪmɪŋ/
dancing	/ˈdænsɪŋ/
gymnastics	/dʒɪmˈnæstɪks/
hiking	/ˈhaɪkɪŋ/
horseback riding	/ˈhɔrsbæk ˈraɪdɪŋ/
ice skating	/ˈaɪs ˈskeɪtɪŋ/
kayaking	/ˈkaɪækɪŋ/
mountain biking	/ˈmaʊntˈn ˈbaɪkɪŋ/
painting	/ˈpeɪntɪŋ/
playing an instrument	/ˈpleɪɪŋ ən ˈɪnstrəmənt/
rollerblading	/ˈroʊlɚˌbleɪdɪŋ/
singing	/ˈsɪŋɪŋ/
surfing	/ˈsɚfɪŋ/

Weather and seasons

autumn/fall	/ˈɔʈəm/, /fɔl/
cloudy	/ˈklaʊdi/
cold	/koʊld/
foggy	/ˈfagi/
hot	/hat/
raining	/ˈreɪnɪŋ/
snowing	/ˈsnoʊɪŋ/
spring	/sprɪŋ/
summer	/ˈsʌmɚ/
sunny	/ˈsʌni/
warm	/wɔrm/
windy	/ˈwɪndi/
winter	/ˈwɪntɚ/

Unit 6 • Delicious!

Food and drinks

banana	/bəˈnænə/
bread	/brɛd/
broccoli	/ˈbrakəli/
cheese	/tʃiz/
chicken	/ˈtʃɪkən/
eggs	/ɛgz/
ham	/hæm/
juice	/dʒus/
pasta	/ˈpastə/
rice	/raɪs/
salmon	/ˈsæmən/
sausage	/ˈsɔsɪdʒ/
shrimp	/ʃrɪmp/
tea	/ti/
tomatoes	/təˈmeɪtoʊz/
tuna	/ˈtunə/
water	/ˈwɔʈɚ/
yogurt	/ˈyoʊgɚt/

Adjectives

clean	/klin/
cold	/koʊld/
delicious	/dɪˈlɪʃəs/
dirty	/ˈdɚti/
disgusting	/dɪsˈgʌstɪŋ/
horrible	/ˈhɔrəbəl/
hot	/hat/
large	/lardʒ/
noisy	/ˈnɔɪzi/
quiet	/ˈkwaɪət/
small	/ˈsmɔl/
wonderful	/ˈwʌndɚfəl/

7 Modern History

Vocabulary • Ordinal numbers, years, dates

1 Listen. Match the numbers you hear to these words. Then listen and repeat.
3.1

fifth
first   *1*
fourth
second
third
thirty-first
twentieth
twenty-second

2 **In pairs, ask and answer.**

1 When is your birthday? *It's on May eighteenth.*
2 What is the date today?

3 **Match the photos (1–8) to the events (a–h).**

a The *Titanic* hits an iceberg. *1*
b Russia sends Laika the dog into space.
c Nelson Mandela leaves prison.
d Prince William marries Kate Middleton.
e Howard Carter discovers Tutankhamen's tomb
   in Egypt.
f The first space vehicle visits Mars.
g In Amsterdam, Anne Frank's family hide
   because of the war.
h People around the world celebrate
   the new millennium.

4 **Match the events in Exercise 3 to these years.**
3.2 **Then listen and check.**

nineteen forty-two	nineteen twelve *a*
nineteen twenty-two	two thousand eleven
two thousand	nineteen fifty-seven
nineteen ninety	two thousand four

**Brain Trainer
Activity 3**
Go to page 64

Reading

1. Look at the article and the photos. Are the photos from the 1960s, '70s or '80s?

2. Read the text. Match the photos (a–e) to the paragraphs (1–3).

3. Read and check your answers to Exercise 2.

4. Read the text again. Complete the events with the correct year.
   3.3

   Event 1 The Beatles' first song in the US *1964*
   Event 2 Twiggy on the cover of *Vogue*
   Event 3 TV in color for the first time
   Event 4 The first men on the moon
   Event 5 The Internet is invented

5. Read the text again. Complete the sentences.
   3.3
   1 "I Want to Hold Your Hand" was a song by *The Beatles*.
   2 In the 1960s people listened to music on the .... or on records.
   3 The colors of .... in the 1960s were very bright.
   4 The first fashion model in Madame Tussaud's was .... .
   5 Some TV shows were in .... after 1967.
   6 The first two men on the moon were .... .

6. What about you? In pairs, ask and answer.
   1 What singers do your parents like?
   2 Do you and your parents like the same music?
   3 Do you have any photos of your parents or grandparents when they were young?

   What singers do your parents like?

   My dad likes Bob Dylan.

Flower Power!

1 What music was popular?
The Beatles were really popular in many countries. Their first song in the US was "I Want to Hold Your Hand" in January 1964. There weren't any MP3 players in the 1960s. There were radios and records!

2 What clothes were in fashion?
Clothes were very different! My grandparents were teenagers in the 1960s, so I have some great photos—look at these pants and shirts! Bright colors and flowers were very popular! Twiggy was the first international fashion model. She appeared on the cover of *Vogue* in the US in 1967, and she also modeled in France, Japan and the UK. She was the first model to appear in Madame Tussaud's wax museum in London.

3 What else?
Well, it was a time of change. Before 1967, TV was boring—it wasn't in color! The year 1969 was exciting! The Concorde's first flight was in April. Then on July 20, Neil Armstrong and Buzz Aldrin were the first men on the moon. In November, the system that became the Internet was invented in the US.

4 Is this an interesting time in history?
Yes, it is! It's fun to learn about different times and find out what people were like.

Grammar • Past simple: *to be*

Affirmative		
I	was	
He/She/It	was	in the café.
You/We/They	were	

Negative		
I	wasn't (was not)	
He/She/It	wasn't (was not)	at home.
You/We/They	weren't (were not)	

Questions		
Was	I	
Was	he/she/it	at school?
Were	you/we/they	

1 Study the grammar table. Copy and complete the table below.

To be

	Present	Past
1	I am	I was
2	She is	*She was*
3	....	We were
4	They aren't	....
5	....	It wasn't
6	You aren't	....
7	Are you?	....
8	....	Was he?

2 Choose the correct options to complete the sentences.

At seven thirty last night …
1 Luke *was / were* at home.
2 Nick *wasn't / weren't* at his grandmother's house.
3 Lucia and Lidia *was / were* at the movies.
4 Luke's parents *wasn't / weren't* at a pizza place.
5 Lidia's dog *was / were* in the backyard.
6 Lucia's friends *wasn't / weren't* in the park.

• There was/There were

Affirmative
There was a radio/some music.
There were some children.

Negative
There wasn't a TV/any music.
There weren't any computers.

Questions and short answers
Was there a phone/any music?
Were there any phones?
Yes, there was. / No, there wasn't.
Yes, there were. / No, there weren't.

Grammar reference page 122

3 Study the grammar table. Complete the rules.

1 We use .... and .... with singular nouns, e.g., *a radio*, to talk about the past.
2 We use .... and .... with plural nouns, e.g., *some computers*, to talk about the past.

4 Complete the questions and write the answers.
1 *Were* there any MP3 players 40 years ago?   ✗
   No, there weren't.
2 *Was* there color TV 20 years ago?   ✓
   Yes, there was.
3 .... there any cell phones 50 years ago?   ✗
4 .... there a man on the moon in 1967?   ✗
5 .... there any DVDs 10 years ago?   ✓
6 .... there Internet 5 years ago?   ✓
7 .... there email 30 years ago?   ✗
8 .... there flowers on clothes in the 1960s?   ✓

5 What about you? **Make sentences about things in your house five years ago. Use these words and/or your own ideas.**

There wasn't a guitar in my house five years ago.

| DVDs | game console | guitar | laptop |
| parrot | rabbit | skateboard | |

Vocabulary • Regular verbs

1 Match the pictures to these words. Then listen, check and repeat.
3.4

answer – answered	ask – asked	call – called
close – closed	invent – invented	like – liked
listen – listened	stop – stopped	study – studied
talk – talked	travel – traveled *1*	work – worked

Word list page 61 **Workbook** page 130

2 Match the phrases (1–4 and a–d) to make spelling rules for regular verbs.

1 Most verbs (e.g., *ask*) *b*
2 Final -*e* (e.g., *like*)
3 Final consonant + -*y* (e.g., *study*)
4 Short vowel + consonant (e.g., *stop*)

a Change *y* to *i*, then add -*ed*
b Add -*ed*
c Double consonant, add -*ed*
d Add -*d*

3 Match the other verbs in Exercise 1 to the spelling rules (1–4).

answer – 1

Pronunciation -*ed* endings

4a Listen to the -*ed* endings of these three regular verbs.
3.5
1 /d/ listened   2 /ɪd/ invented   3 /t/ talked

b Listen to these Past simple regular verbs. Which ending
3.6 does each verb have: /d/, /ɪd/ or /t/?

1 started   2 watched   3 opened   4 asked   5 studied
6 wanted   7 worked   8 liked   9 called

c Listen again. Check your answers.
3.6

5 Complete the text with these words in the past. Then listen and check.
3.7

answer	ask	call
~~invent~~	like	listen
study	talk	travel
work		

Alexander Graham Bell ¹*invented* the telephone in the 1870s. First, he ².... inventions from other inventors. Then he ³.... with his friend, Mr. Watson. On June 2, 1872, Bell ⁴.... Mr. Watson and ⁵.... to him. Mr. Watson ⁶...., and Bell ⁷...., "Do you understand what I say?" "Yes," ⁸.... Mr. Watson. Bell's words ⁹.... sixteen kilometers. It was the first "long-distance" phone call. People ¹⁰.... Bell's idea. The phone changed their lives.

6 Complete the sentences with verbs from Exercise 1.

1 Can I *ask* you a question?
2 Please, can you .... the door?
3 I can't .... the question.
4 Do you .... your new camera?

7 Write three sentences about yesterday. Use the verbs from Exercise 1.

I called Irina yesterday.

Brain Trainer Activity 4
Go to page 64

Speaking and **Listening**

1. **Look at the photo. What things does Julia's grandma have?**

2. **Listen and read the conversation. Are the**
3.8 **statements true (T) or false (F)?**

1 Julia's grandma is reading a book. *F*
2 Julia's grandma lived with her sister for a year while her husband was in Vietnam.
3 Julia's grandpa mailed a lot of letters.
4 Julia's grandpa often called Julia's grandma.
5 It was cheap to make a phone call.
6 The phone booth wasn't near the house.
7 Julia's grandparents moved to where they live now two years ago.
8 Julia's grandparents watched TV every evening.
9 They liked pop music.

3. **Act out the conversation in groups of three.**

Julia	Hello, Grandma! Sorry I didn't visit you last weekend. What are you doing?
Grandma	I'm reading some old letters from your grandpa. You know, I lived with my sister for two years while he was in Vietnam. He mailed a letter to me every week … but he didn't call me very often.
Julia	Why not?
Grandpa	Because it was expensive!
Grandma	And the phone was in a phone booth three kilometers away!
Julia	What a pain!
Grandma	Then I moved here in the 1970s. That was about forty years ago.
Grandpa	I remember. In those days, we listened to the radio every evening.
Julia	Really? What was your favorite music?
Grandma	We loved rock'n'roll.

Say it in your language …
What a pain!

4 Look back at the conversation. Who says what?

1 I didn't visit you last weekend. *Julia*
2 I lived with my sister for two years.
3 I moved here in the 1970s.
4 That was forty years ago.
5 In those days, we listened to the radio.

5 Read the phrases for talking about the past.

Past-time expressions
last weekend
for two years
in the 1970s
forty years ago
in those days

6 Listen to the conversations. Act out the conversations in pairs.

3.9

Steven Where were you ¹ last weekend?
Were you at home?
Nina No, I wasn't. I was ² at my grandparents' house.

Jason I wasn't at school ¹ yesterday morning.
Sonia Really? Why not?
Jason Because I was ² sick.

7 Work in pairs. Replace the words in purple in Exercise 6 with these words. Act out the conversations.

Where were you yesterday?

I was at a friend's house.

1 last night / last week / last Friday

2 at the movies / in Hawaii / at school

1 yesterday afternoon / last Thursday / three days ago

2 at the doctor's office / at the dentist's office / at home in bed

8 Act out the conversation again with your own words and ideas.

Grammar • Past simple regular: affirmative and negative

Affirmative	
I/You/He/She/It/ We/They	listened. danced. studied. traveled.

Negative	
I/You/He/She/It/ We/They	didn't (did not) listen. didn't (did not) dance. didn't (did not) study. didn't (did not) travel.

Grammar reference page 122

1 Study the grammar table. Answer the questions to complete the rules.

1 Is the third person (He/She/It) different in the Past simple?
2 How do we make the Past simple negative?

2 Complete the sentences with the Past simple affirmative.

1 Yesterday she .... (clean up) her room.
2 We .... (carry) the computer to the classroom.
3 The actors .... (dance) in that movie.
4 Our dog .... (jump) in the car this morning.
5 My friends and I .... (walk) to school last week.
6 We .... (watch) a DVD last night.
7 The bus .... (stop) near the museum.

3 Put the sentences in Exercise 2 in the negative form.

1 *Yesterday she didn't clean up her room.*

4 Complete the text with these verbs in the Past simple.

clean up	get	not help	not like
not watch	play	~~stay~~	want

Last night my parents were out, so I ¹ *stayed* at home with my brother, Harry. I ² .... the living room, but Harry ³ .... me. Next, I ⁴ .... games with him, but he ⁵ .... the games. Then he ⁶ .... to watch *Jaws*, a scary movie about a shark. We ⁷ .... it for long. When Mom and Dad ⁸ .... home, my brother and I were behind the sofa!

Reading

1 Look at the names (1–6). Can you match them to the photos (a–f)?

1 *Jaws* 4 *ET*
2 *Grease* 5 Andy Warhol
3 ABBA 6 Michael Jackson

Travel Back in Time!

Welcome to the Time Tunnels at **The Max Museum of Modern Culture!**

In the first Time Tunnel, you can relive the culture of the '70s. This was a time of freedom for women and young people in America and Western Europe. Andy Warhol was a famous pop artist. His career started in the '60s, but he was popular in the '70s because his work was fresh and modern.

At that time, people watched exciting movies like *Jaws*, *Star Wars* and *Grease*. In the evening, people enjoyed disco music. They danced to ABBA, the European superstars from Sweden. Some movie posters and record covers from the '70s are pieces of art now.

In the second Time Tunnel, you can visit the '80s. American culture was "cool" in that decade; many people liked fast food and Hollywood blockbuster movies like *ET* and *Wall Street*. People worked long hours, and some young people wanted a lot of money, but others didn't like this culture of "Me, me, me." Graffiti art was one way to show that they were angry.

In the '80s, people enjoyed some great pop music—for example, Madonna and Michael Jackson. Their videos and stage shows were also a type of art.

Key Words		
tunnel	culture	freedom
fresh	blockbuster	angry

2 Read and check your answers to Exercise 1.

3 Read the text quickly. Are these people and things from the '70s or '80s Time Tunnel?
3.10

a Graffiti art *'80s Time Tunnel*
b Andy Warhol
c *Wall Street*
d Madonna
e *Star Wars*
f ABBA

4 Read the text again. Answer the questions.
3.10

1 What type of museum is it?
   It is a museum of modern culture.
2 Who was Andy Warhol?
3 Which Swedish band was famous for disco music?
4 What were two examples of American culture?
5 Why was graffiti art popular in the '80s?

Listening

1 Listen to three people from The Max Museum.
3.11 Match each speaker to the thing he/she does.

Speaker 1
Speaker 2
Speaker 3
a take photographs
b sell tickets
c work in the gift shop

2 Listen again and find these things.
3.11

1 names of two famous people
2 three colors
3 a number

3 What about you? **Imagine you are in the year 2030. In pairs, say what the year 2014 was like.**

Writing • An essay

1 Read the Writing File.

Writing File Punctuation 2

- We use **periods (.)** at the end of a sentence.

- We use **commas (,)** to make a pause in the middle of a sentence, e.g., before *but*.

- We use **question marks (?)** at the end of a question. Be careful! We don't use question marks at the beginning of a question.

- We use **exclamation points (!)** to express surprise.

2 Read Jason's essay. What punctuation (1–5) is missing?

When I Was Young

The "noughties" (2000–2009) were a good time to be young [1] [] There were some great TV shows for kids, like the Japanese cartoon *Yu-Gi-Oh*. *Yu-Gi-Oh* was about Yugi, a high school student with a Pharaoh's spirit. I loved it!

There were also some good movies a few years ago. The Harry Potter movies were very popular, and I was a big fan. I didn't see them at the theater, but I watched them on DVD a lot of times [2] [...] My favorite character was Ron Weasley [3] [...] but I didn't like Lord Voldemort.

Was there any good music in the noughties [4] [...] I think so. I liked Linkin Park [5] [...] but music in the twenty-tens is better. My Chemical Romance and The Wanted are amazing!

Jason, Australia

3 Read the essay again. Answer the questions.

1 When were the "noughties"?
  The "noughties" were from 2000 to 2009.
2 Which country was the show *Yu-Gi-Oh* from?
3 Was Jason a Harry Potter fan?
4 Who was his favorite character?
5 Which was his favorite band in the "noughties"?
6 What bands does Jason like now?

4 Rewrite the sentences with commas (if necessary) and a period or a question mark.

1 The song was old but it was very popular
  The song was old, but it was very popular.
2 Who was in the Harry Potter movies
3 How old were you in 2010
4 We watched TV yesterday afternoon
5 I liked *Pokémon* but I didn't like *Yu-Gi-Oh*

5 Think about when you were young. Take notes about these things. Give reasons.

1 TV shows you liked – and why
2 movies you liked – and why
3 singers and bands you liked – and why

6 Write an essay titled "When I Was Young." Use "My essay" and your notes from Exercise 5.

My essay

Paragraph 1
1 Say what time you are writing about.
2 Say what shows you liked.

Paragraph 2
3 Say what movies you liked.

Paragraph 3
4 Say what music you liked.
5 Compare it with music you like now.

Remember!
- Use punctuation correctly.
- Use the vocabulary in this unit.
- Check your grammar, spelling and punctuation.

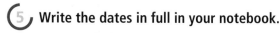

Refresh Your Memory!

Grammar • Review

1 Complete the text with *was/wasn't* or *were/weren't*.

• Which countries ¹ *were* in the "Space Race"?

In the 1950s and '60s, Russia and America ² ....
in a "Space Race." The first man in space ³ ....
Yuri Gagarin from Russia.

• Which country ⁴ .... first on the moon?

The first rocket on the moon ⁵ .... American. It was
the Russian Luna 2 in 1959, but there weren't any
people in this rocket. The first men on the moon
⁶ .... from Russia. They were from America.
The date ⁷ .... July 20, 1969. Buzz Aldrin and Neil
Armstrong ⁸ .... on the moon for 21 hours.

2 Make sentences with *There was/were* or *There wasn't/weren't*.

1 an MP3 player on the table
   There was an MP3 player on the table.
2 not any songs on the MP3 player
3 some DVDs next to a laptop
4 not a car in the garage
5 a cell phone on the chair
6 some text messages on the phone

3 Make sentences with the Past simple.

1 Jake / visit / his friend in the hospital yesterday
   Jake visited his friend in the hospital yesterday.
2 Angelina / play / soccer with her brother
3 We / call / our grandparents last night
4 Sam and Sara / study / for their math test
5 The students / answer / the teacher's questions
6 The car / stop / near the park

4 Correct the sentences.

1 Howard Carter discovered Tutankhamen's
   tomb in Greece. (Egypt)
   He didn't discover Tutankhamen's tomb
   in Greece. He discovered it in Egypt.
2 The first space vehicle visited Mars in 2012. (2004)
3 People celebrated the millennium in 1998. (2000)
4 Alexander Graham Bell invented the MP3
   player. (telephone)
5 Anne Frank's family lived in Paris. (Amsterdam)

Vocabulary • Review

5 Write the dates in full in your notebook.

1 4/20/1982
   April twentieth, nineteen eighty-two
2 3/10/2030
3 8/3/1861
4 1/21/2018
5 10/2/2003
6 8/1/1999

6 Match the verbs (1–4) to the correct Past simple spelling rules (a–d).

1 dance / love
2 chop / plan
3 play / clean
4 study / hurry

a add -*ed*
b change -*y* to -*i*, add -*ed*
c double the consonant, add -*ed*
d add -*d*

Speaking • Review

7 Complete the conversations with a past time
3.12 word. Then listen and check.

last	ago	yesterday

Adam Where's Mom?
Erin I don't know. She was here
          half an hour ¹ .... .

Ivan Where were you ² .... night?
          Were you at the gym?
Eva   No, I wasn't. I was at home.

Dina Why didn't you go to school ³ .... ?
Paulo Because I was at the doctor's office.

Dictation

8 Listen and write in your notebook.
3.13

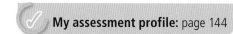

✓ **My assessment profile:** page 144

Twenty-Four Hours in the Life of a Roman Child

The day started with breakfast. For rich Romans, there was bread, fish, meat, fruit and honey. Slaves prepared and served the food. For poor Romans, breakfast was different. They had bread with water.

Then it was time to go to school. School started really early—before sunrise—and it got out late! Schools weren't big. There was usually one tutor and a small group of children. At school, children studied reading, writing and math. They used small stones to do math problems. They practiced writing on wax tablets—they scratched the words onto the wax with a pointed stick.

Most children finished school when they were 10 or 11, but some children continued to a "Grammar school." Here they studied Latin, Greek, grammar and literature. They also practiced public speaking. Some children studied at home. Their teachers were the family's slaves. The slaves were often smart and well-educated, and they were good teachers.

After school, children played with toys at home. The boys often played war games and practiced fighting. Some Roman toys are very similar to modern toys. Roman children played with dolls, hoops, kites and stilts.

Reading

1 **Read the text quickly. What do you think it is about?**

a Roman food
b Roman daily life
c Education in Rome today

2 **Read the text again. Answer the questions.**

3.14

1 What did rich people have for breakfast?
   People had bread, fish, meat, fruit and honey.
2 Who prepared the food for rich people?
3 Were schools big or small?
4 What did children study at school?
5 Who taught children at home?
6 What did children play with at home?

3 **Do some research into the daily life of a child from ancient Egypt. Find the answers to these questions:**

• When did he/she get up?
• When did he/she go to bed?
• What did he/she eat?
• What did he/she do?

4 **Write a short paragraph about the daily life of an ancient Egyptian child in your notebook. Use your notes from Exercise 3 to help you.**

Travel

Vocabulary • Means of transportation

Grammar
Past simple irregular:
affirmative and negative;
Past simple: questions

Vocabulary
Means of transportation;
Clothes

Speaking
Talking on the phone

Writing
A travel diary

Word list page 61
Workbook page 131

1 Match the vehicles in the picture to these words. Then listen, check and repeat.

3.15

bike
boat
bus
canoe
car *1*
helicopter
motorcycle
plane
scooter
subway
train
truck
van

2 Which means of transportation from Exercise 1
3.16 can you hear? Listen and say.

1 *It's a boat.*

3 Where do you usually use each means
of transportation? Complete the list.

1 **on land:**   2 **on water:**   3 **in the air:**
car, … .   *boat, … .*   *plane, … .*

4 Match the verbs to the nouns.

1 take   a a plane
2 sail   b a train
3 drive   c a bike, a motorcycle
4 fly   d a boat
5 ride   e a car

5 In pairs, make up an unusual route from your
home to another country. You must use at least
five different means of transportation.

> First, we ride our bikes
> to the bus stop. Next, we take a
> bus to the river. Then we …

Brain Trainer
Activity 4
Go to page 65

Reading

1 Look at the extracts (a–c) from *Around the World in Eighty Days* by Jules Verne. Guess: what is it about?

a Phileas Fogg can't find his bag. Is it in France? Is it in China? He travels to 80 countries. But where is his bag?

b It is 1872. Phileas Fogg's friends say, "No one can travel around the world in 80 days." "I can!" says Phileas Fogg. And his adventure begins.

c Phileas Fogg works at a train station. He meets many people from different countries. He hears 80 stories from 80 places around the world, but he never travels.

2 Read and check your ideas to Exercise 1.

3 Read the text quickly. Put the events
3.17 in the correct order.

a Passepartout gets a bag for Phileas Fogg.
b Phileas Fogg goes into his house.
c Phileas Fogg leaves the Club. *1*
d Phileas Fogg and Passepartout get on a train.
e Phileas Fogg says goodbye to his friends.
f Phileas Fogg sees his friends at the station.
g Phileas Fogg gives his bag to Passepartout.

4 Read the text again. Answer the questions.
3.17
1 Where are Phileas Fogg's friends at the beginning of the extract? *They are at the Club.*
2 Where does Phileas Fogg live?
3 Phileas Fogg asks Passepartout for two things. What are they?
4 What does Phileas Fogg put inside the bag?
5 Where are Phileas Fogg's friends at the end of the extract?
6 What time do Phileas Fogg and Passepartout leave Charing Cross Station?

5 What about you? In pairs, ask and answer.
1 Do you like traveling?
2 Imagine you are traveling around the world in 80 days. What do you want to put in your suitcase?

Around the World in Eighty Days

At 7:25, Phileas Fogg said good night to his friends and left the Club. At 7:50, he opened the door of his house in Savile Row and went in.

"Mr. Fogg? Is that you?" said Passepartout.

"We must go to Charing Cross Station immediately. I want to make a trip around the world."

Passepartout didn't understand him.

"Around the world?" he asked.

"In eighty days," said Phileas Fogg. "We must go now. Now!"

"But your bags?"

"I need one small bag. Bring my coat. Wear strong shoes. Move!"

At eight o'clock, Passepartout was ready with a small bag. "A quiet life," he thought. "Where is my quiet life?"

Phileas Fogg didn't have a lot of things for the trip. He took the bag from Passepartout and put a lot of money, and a train and ship schedule, into it. Then he gave the bag to Passepartout.

At the station, Phileas Fogg saw his five friends from the Club.

"You're here to say goodbye? That's kind," he said.

At 8:40, Phileas Fogg and Passepartout got on the train, and at 8:45 the train started.

Grammar • Past simple irregular: affirmative and negative

Base	Affirmative	Negative
buy	bought	didn't (did not) buy
do	did	didn't (did not) do
get	got	didn't (did not) get
give	gave	didn't (did not) give
go	went	didn't (did not) go
have	had	didn't (did not) have
put	put	didn't (did not) put
take	took	didn't (did not) take
think	thought	didn't (did not) think
understand	understood	didn't (did not) understand

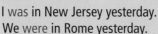

Watch Out!
They went to Paris last month.
You didn't go to Orlando last month.
BUT:
I was in New Jersey yesterday.
We were in Rome yesterday.

He wasn't in Rome yesterday.
They weren't in New Jersey yesterday.

Go to page 141 **for a full list of irregular Past simple verbs**

Grammar reference page 124

1. **Study the grammar table. Complete the rule.**

For the Past simple negative form, we put the word .... before the base verb.

2. **Are these Past simple verbs regular (R) or irregular (I)?**

buy – bought /	drink – drank	give – gave
live – lived	say – said	see – saw
study – studied	visit – visited	work – worked

3. **Complete the text below with the Past simple.**

I ¹ *went* (go) downtown with my friend Elizabeth last weekend. We ² .... (see) a great movie at the theater. After the movie, we ³ .... (go) shopping. I ⁴ .... (buy) a new game for my game console. My friend ⁵ .... (get) a book about computers. Then we ⁶ .... (eat) some pizza at a pizza place. At seven o'clock, we ⁷ .... (take) the bus home. We ⁸ .... (have) a great day.

4. **Rewrite the verbs from Exercise 3 in the Past simple negative.**

1 *I didn't go.*

5. **Complete the article.**

True Stories: I Changed My Life

Jane Fletcher before   Jane Fletcher now

Jane Fletcher is healthier and happier today. Why? She changed her life.

Now she ¹ *walks* (walk) to work every day, but two years ago she ² *didn't walk* (not walk) to work; she ³ *went* (go) by car. Now she ⁴ .... (have) cereal for breakfast, but two years ago she ⁵ .... (not have) cereal for breakfast; she ⁶ .... (have) cake. Now she ⁷ .... (go to bed) at ten o'clock, but two years ago she ⁸ .... (not go to bed) at ten o'clock; she ⁹ .... (go to bed) at midnight. Now she ¹⁰ .... (ride) her bike in the park on the weekend, but two years ago, she ¹¹ .... (not ride) her bike; she drove her car downtown on the weekend.

6. **What about you? Write three true statements about something you changed in your life.**

Vocabulary • Clothes

1 Match the pictures to these words. Then listen, check and repeat.

3.18

boots	coat	dress *1*	hat
jeans	pajamas	pants	sandals
scarf	shoes	shorts	skirt
sneakers	sweater	T-shirt	

Word list page 61
Workbook page 131

2 Copy and put the clothes words in Exercise 1 into the correct category. Then listen, check and repeat.

3.19

a top half of body
   coat, ... , ...
b bottom half of body
   .... , ... , ... , ...
c whole body
   .... , ...
d feet
   .... , ... , ... , ...
e head and neck
   .... , ...

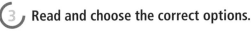

3 Read and choose the correct options.

In winter I usually wear ¹ *jeans / shorts*, a ² *T-shirt / sweater* and ³ *sandals / boots*. When I go outside, I always wear a ⁴ *skirt / coat*, and sometimes I have a ⁵ *hat / scarf* around my neck, too. Today it's very hot and sunny, so I'm wearing a summer ⁶ *sweater / dress*. My sister isn't feeling well, so she's still in bed, and she's wearing her ⁷ *sneakers / pajamas*.

4 Listen. Who is Ben's sister?

3.20

   a Dolly   b Molly   c Holly

5 Choose one person in the class. Describe his/her clothes to your partner. Can your partner guess who the person is?

**Brain Trainer
Activity 5**
Go to page 65

Speaking and Listening

1 Look at the photos. Answer the questions.

1 Is Julia happy or sad?
2 What is Nick doing?

2 Listen and read the conversation.
3.21 Answer the questions.

1 Who is Mr. Davies? *Nick's dad*
2 Who does Julia want to speak to?
3 Where is Julia?
4 What does Julia want to do on Saturday?
5 Where did Julia wear her scarf yesterday?
6 What does Julia want to do this evening?

3 Act out the conversation in groups of three.

Mr. Davies	Hello?
Julia	Hi, is this Nick?
Mr. Davies	No, it isn't. This is his dad. Who's this?
Julia	Hi, Mr. Davies, it's Julia. Can I speak to Nick, please?
Mr. Davies	Hello, Julia! Hold on ... Nick! Just a minute ... here he is.
Nick	Hi, Julia! Where are you?
Julia	I'm at home. Listen, I can't find my favorite purple scarf, and I want to wear it on Saturday. Did I leave it at your house?
Nick	I don't know. Did you wear it to school yesterday?
Julia	Yes, I did. But it's not there. I checked this morning. Can I come to your house this evening? I want to look for it.
Nick	Sure. See you later. Bye!
Julia	Bye!

Say it in your language ...

Just a minute.
Listen, ...

4 Look back at the conversation. How does Julia ask to speak to Nick? How does Mr. Davies ask Julia to wait?

5 Read the phrases for talking on the phone.

Talking on the phone
Hi / Hello, is this … ?
Who's this?
It's … .
Can I speak to … , please?
Hold on.
Just a minute.
Here he is.
See you later.
Bye!

Pronunciation Sounding polite

6a Listen. Who is more polite, Emma or Valerie?

3.22
Henry	Hello.
Emma	Hello, is this Frank?
Henry	No, it's Henry.
Emma	Hi, Henry, it's Emma. Can I speak to Frank, please?
Henry	Hello.
Valerie	Hello, Henry, it's Valerie.
Henry	Hi, Valerie.
Valerie	Can I speak to Frank, please?

b Listen again and repeat.
3.22

7 Listen to the conversations. Act out
3.23 the conversations in pairs.

Nick	Hello.
Leo	Hi, Nick, it's Leo. Can I speak to Ted, please?
Nick	Hold on.
Mrs. Green	Hello.
Monica	Hello, is this Rebecca?
Mrs. Green	No, it isn't. This is her mother.
Monica	Oh, sorry. Can I speak to Rebecca, please?
Mrs. Green	Of course. Here she is.

Grammar • Past simple: questions

Questions and short answers
Did I/you/he/she/it/we/they read the book?
Yes, I/you/he/she/it/we/they did.
No, I/you/he/she/it/we/they didn't.

Wh questions
Where did I/you/he/she/it/we/they go yesterday?
I went to the movies.

Grammar reference page 124

1 Study the grammar table. Complete the rule.

> We make Past simple questions with …. + *I / you / he / she / it / we / they* + verb.

2 Read Jamie's answers and complete
3.24 the questions. Then listen and check.

1 Where *did you go* (go) last weekend?
  I went to Seattle.
2 How …. there? (get)
  I flew there.
3 What …. in Seattle? (do)
  I climbed the Space Needle.
4 When …. ? (leave)
  I left on Sunday evening.
5 …. home? (fly)
  No, I didn't. I came home by bus.

3 Make questions and answers.

A you / meet / Jane / yesterday?
B I / have / lunch with her. Then / we / go / to the movies
A Did you meet Jane yesterday?
B Yes, I did. I had lunch with her. Then …
A What / movie / you / see?
B We / see / the new Kristen Stewart movie
A you / enjoy it?
B I / not like / it. I / think / it / be / really boring

4 In pairs, find out about your partner's favorite vacation. Use these ideas.

do some painting	go kayaking
go rollerblading	go to museums
listen to music	meet with friends
play tennis	stay in a hotel

Reading

1. **Look at the photo. Where do you think these people live?**

   a in a village   b in a tent   c in a big city

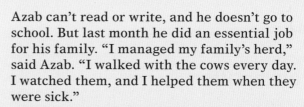

AZAB'S JOURNEY

Azab is thirteen years old. He lives in Niger, in West Africa, but he doesn't live in a village or a town, and his family doesn't have a house. Azab is a Wodaabe nomad. There are more than 40,000 Wodaabe people in Niger. They live in simple tents, and they travel every two or three days. They follow the rain and move to places with water and grass for their cattle. The cows are very important for the Wodaabe people because cows' milk is their main food. They make yogurt and butter with the milk, and when they are near a village, they sell the milk and buy other food.

Azab can't read or write, and he doesn't go to school. But last month he did an essential job for his family. "I managed my family's herd," said Azab. "I walked with the cows every day. I watched them, and I helped them when they were sick."

Last year Azab's family traveled more than 3,000 kilometers around West Africa. "There was no rain," said Azab. "We went from one place to another place. We didn't find food and we were hungry. It was a very difficult time."

Key Words		
nomad	to follow	cattle
essential	to manage	herd

2. **Read and check your answer to Exercise 1.**

3. **Read the text quickly. Choose the correct description.**
   3.25

   Wodaabe nomads …
   a live in villages in Niger and sell cows.
   b travel around West Africa and don't have houses.
   c move to different places because they don't have cows.

4. **Read the text again. Answer the questions.**
   3.25
   1 How old is Azab? *Azab is thirteen years old.*
   2 How many Wodaabe people live in Niger?
   3 Why do they move to different places?
   4 What do they usually eat?
   5 What did Azab do last month?
   6 Why was life difficult for Azab's family last year?

Listening

1. **Listen to Rose's conversation with Erik.**
   3.26 **Answer the questions.**

   1 Did Rose have a good day or a bad day?
   2 Where is she now?

2. **Listen again. Are the statements true (T)**
   3.26 **or false (F)?**

   1 Rose got up late because she didn't hear her alarm clock. *T*
   2 Rose took the bus to school.
   3 Rose liked her trip to school today.
   4 Rose got to school late.
   5 Rose's teacher was angry because she didn't have her homework.
   6 Rose is doing her homework now.

Writing • A travel diary

1 Read the Writing File.

2 Read the travel diary. Match the paragraphs (A–C) to the descriptions (1–3).

1 Summary of the day
2 Description of the Taj Mahal
3 Description of the journey to Agra

My Indian Diary by Jamie Weller

Monday

A Today we traveled 200 kilometers from New Delhi to the Taj Mahal in Agra. We went by bus, and the trip took three hours. It was very hot, and there were a lot of people, but we enjoyed it.

B When we arrived at the Taj Mahal, we were amazed. It looks beautiful in photographs, but it's even more beautiful in real life! Our guide talked about the history of the building, and then we walked around it.

C We returned to New Delhi in the evening. We were very tired when we got back to our hotel, but it was a fantastic day. The Taj Mahal is awesome!

3 Read the diary again. Answer the questions.

1 How far is Agra from New Delhi?
   It is 200 kilometers.
2 Did Jamie like traveling on the bus?
3 What did they do when they arrived at the Taj Mahal?
4 Did they stay in Agra on Monday night?

4 Read the text and divide it into paragraphs.

Paragraph 1   Description of the market
Paragraph 2   Description of the Lodi Gardens
Paragraph 3   Summary of the day

Tuesday

We got up early today and walked to the Dilli Haat market. The market is interesting. You can buy a lot of different things there. I loved the clothes, and my sister liked the food! We took a bus from the market to Lodi Gardens. They are really beautiful. We had a picnic and watched the birds. I loved the shopping in the morning, and the gardens were amazing.

5 Imagine you are on a trip. Answer the questions.

1 What did you see?
2 What did you buy?
3 Did you enjoy the experience? Why?/Why not?

Places to visit
museums / interesting buildings / the beach / an amusement park / a palace / a park / gardens

Adjectives
Positive: interesting / amazing / great
Negative: noisy / horrible / dirty

Things to do
buy souvenirs / swim in the ocean / visit museums

6 Write your travel diary. Use "My diary" and your notes from Exercise 5.

My diary

Paragraph 1
Yesterday / Last summer I went to … .
We went by bus / train / plane.
We saw … .
Paragraph 2
I / My sister / My mother bought … .
Paragraph 3
It was interesting / great / horrible … .

Remember!
- Divide your writing into paragraphs.
- Use the vocabulary in this unit.
- Check your grammar, spelling and punctuation.

Refresh Your Memory!

Grammar • Review

1) Choose the correct options.

1 I *didn't understand / not understood* the homework, so I *didn't do / not did* it.
2 Mary *speak / spoke* to Jason yesterday.
3 We *saw / see* your cousin on his motorcycle this morning.
4 He *go / went* to Miami by plane.
5 My friends *didn't / don't* take the bus to school yesterday; they *take / took* the subway.

2) Complete the text with the Past simple form of the verbs.

Last Saturday I ¹ *had* (have) a picnic with my uncle and my cousins. We ² .... (drink) fruit smoothies, and we ³ .... (have) some delicious sandwiches. After the food, we all ⁴ .... (sing) songs together. It ⁵ .... (be) a wonderful day.

3) Put the words in the correct order to make questions.

1 my message / Did / you / to Tom / give / ?
   Did you give my message to Tom?
2 you / at the supermarket / did / What / buy / ?
3 your friends / at midnight / leave / the party / Did / ?
4 books / How many / read / last year / you / did / ?
5 Sarah / on the math test / get / 100% / Did / ?
6 Where / go / did / on vacation / you / ?

4) Make questions and answers.

1 you / go to the park / yesterday?
   No. I / go to the gym
   Did you go to the park yesterday?
   No, I didn't. I went to the gym.
2 you / play tennis with Peter / at the gym?
   No. we / go swimming
3 you and Peter / have lunch / at the café?
   No. we / have lunch / at Peter's house
4 you / take the bus home / after lunch?
   No. I / walk / home
5 you / do your homework / in the afternoon?
   No. I / listen / to music
6 you / send an email to Eva / in the evening?
   No. I / call Eva

Vocabulary • Review

5) Complete the transportation sentences with the missing letters.

1 *Cars*, t _ _ _ _ _ and v _ _ _ d _ _ _ _ on land.
2 B _ _ _ _ s _ _ _ on water.
3 P _ _ _ _ _ and h _ _ _ _ _ _ _ _ _ _ f _ _ in the air.

6) Read and match.

1 You wear these on your feet when you play sports.   a dress
2 You wear these on your feet in the summer.   b sandals
3 You wear this on the top half of your body.   c scarf
                                                  d sneakers
4 You wear them in bed.
5 Girls wear this.   e sweater
6 You wear this on your head.   f pants
7 You wear this around your neck.   g hat
8 You wear them on your legs.   h pajamas

Speaking • Review

7) Complete the phone conversation with these words. Then listen and check.
3.27

Bye	Can I speak	Hold on
~~is this~~	See you later	Who's speaking

Tina Hello.
James Hello, ¹ *is this* Maddy?
Tina No, it's Tina. ² ...., please?
James Hi, Tina, it's James. ³ .... to Maddy, please?
Tina Sure. ⁴ ..... Here she is.
Maddy Hi, James.
James Hi, Maddy. I'm bored. Can I come over to your house this afternoon?
Maddy Yes, of course.
James OK, then. ⁵ ..... Bye.
Maddy ⁶ .... .

Dictation

8) Listen and write in your notebook.
3.28

 My assessment profile: page 145

Phiona Mutesi's Profile

Age	Home country
17	Uganda

City

Kampala

Phiona's Journey

Phiona Mutesi is from a poor part of Uganda, and she left school when she was 8 years old. The following year, when she was 9, she joined a chess club at her church. Her brothers went there, and she followed them. At first she didn't know what chess was, but she liked the chess pieces! She practiced every evening at home with her brothers, and she soon became very good at the game.

In 2007 Phiona entered her first tournament. She was 11 years old, and she played chess against people ages 18, 19 and 20. Some people laughed at her because her clothes were simple, and she was poor. But she won the tournament, and people stopped laughing.

In 2009, when she was 13 years old, Phiona Mutesi made her first trip to another country. She traveled on a plane from her home in Uganda to Juba in South Sudan to play chess in an international tournament with children from 16 other countries. She won all her games, and she won the girls' title.

Now she is the No. 2 chess player in Uganda. Her teacher, Robert Katende, says, "In chess, it does not matter where you come from. Only where you put the pieces."

Reading

1 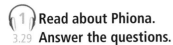 **Read about Phiona.**
3.29 **Answer the questions.**

1 When did Phiona leave school?
   When she was 8 years old.
2 Where did she learn to play chess?
3 How did she become good at the game?
4 Why did some people laugh at Phiona?
5 Did Phiona win the chess tournament in 2007?
6 When did she go to Juba?
7 How many countries did the children at the tournament come from?

Class discussion

- Is there a chess club in your city, town or school?
- What do you like to do after school?
- Imagine Phiona's trip to Juba. What things were new or unusual for her?

9 Technology Time

Grammar
Be going to; Present continuous for future arrangements

Vocabulary
Technology;
Technology phrases

Speaking
Asking for information

Writing
A story

Word list page 61
Workbook page 132

Vocabulary • Technology

1 Match the objects in the photos to these words. Then listen, check and repeat.

3.30

blog
broadband
digital radio
e-reader   *1*
flash drive
IM (instant messaging)
interactive whiteboard
netbook
screen
smart phone
social networking site
Wi-Fi

2 Complete the sentences with words from Exercise 1.

1 I did my homework on my home computer, then I took it to school on a f*lash drive*.
2 I don't use a laptop. I use a n .... because it's smaller.
3 You can talk to a lot of friends and share photos on a s .... .
4 It's faster to go on the Internet with b ..... .
5 The s .... on a cell phone is very small.
6 You can use a W .... Internet connection in many different places.
7 My dad always listens to the sports news on his d .... .

3 Read the definition and say the word.

1 Teachers sometimes write on this in the classroom. *interactive whiteboard*
2 This is a fast way to send short messages.
3 This is a cell phone which has email and an MP3 player.
4 This isn't a paper book. It's electronic.
5 This is an online diary.

4 In pairs, ask and answer about technology.

Do you use IM?

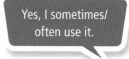
Yes, I sometimes/ often use it.

Brain Trainer
Activity 3
Go to page 66

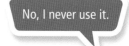
No, I never use it.

Reading

1 Look at the text and the photos. What do you think the text is about?

a The future of novels
b E-readers vs cell phones
c The future of reading

2 Read the text and check your answer to Exercise 1.

3 Read the text again. Add the words or sentences
3.31 (a–c) to the paragraphs (1–3).

a Why don't you write one today?
b They're going to be waterproof too, so we can read in the bathtub!
c phone texts, instant messages and short messages on social networking sites.

4 Read the text again. Complete the sentences
3.31 with one word from the text.

1 These days people often read text on a *screen*.
2 Soon, e-readers are going to .... .
3 E-readers with flexible screens are .... .
4 In the future, e-books can have 3-D .... .
5 "Keitai" are popular in .... .
6 You read "keitai" novels on a .... .
7 Twitter novels are very .... .

5 What about you? In pairs, ask and answer.

1 Do you read paper books or e-books?
2 Which is better, an e-book or a paper book?
3 Can you write a Twitter novel?

> Do you read paper books, e-books or no books?

> I read paper books. I love reading!

---

e-reading!

← → C ⌂

E-Reading!

1 We use computers all the time, and we read text on a screen every day—[1].... Many people use their cell phone to read, and some have e-readers. What do you use? What are you going to use in the future?

2 E-readers are going to change in the future. We know that producers of e-readers are going to give them flexible screens so they're soft and easy to carry. [2].... But what are we going to see after that? Imagine a new generation of e-readers that can read you a story, e-books that can change color, e-books with 3-D pictures. All of them are going to be possible.

3 What about books for cell phones? In Japan, "keitai" are popular. These are very short novels for people to read on their cell phones. Even teenagers can become writers of "keitai" novels. Many people also like the new fashion for Twitter novels. These are only 140 characters long—that's shorter than this paragraph! [3]....

Grammar • Be going to

Affirmative		
I	'm (am)	going to read an e-book on the weekend.
You/We/They	're (are)	
He/She/It	's (is)	

Negative		
I	'm not (am not)	going to use IM this evening.
You/We/They	aren't (are not)	
He/She/It	isn't (is not)	

Questions and short answers		
Am	I	going to buy a laptop tomorrow?
Are	you/we/they	
Is	he/she/it	

Yes, I am. / No, I'm not.
Yes, you/we/they are. / No, you/we/they aren't.
Yes, he/she/it is. / No, he/she/it isn't.

Watch Out!

Use *be going to* with these expressions:

tomorrow, next week, next month, next year, soon

Grammar reference page 126

1 Study the grammar table. Complete the rules.

1 Before *going to,* we use the verb ..... .
2 To make the negative, we add .... before *going to.*
3 In the question form, the first words are ..... .

2 Complete the sentences with the affirmative of *be going to.*

1 I *'m going to stay* (stay) with my grandparents this summer.
2 Ella .... (climb) Sydney Harbor Bridge next month.
3 Nina's family .... (fly) to Rio de Janeiro on the weekend.
4 Omar and his mom .... (visit) the Leaning Tower of Pisa tomorrow.
5 My dad .... (run) a marathon next week.

3 The sentences in Exercise 2 are false. Rewrite them in the negative.

1 *I'm not going to stay with my grandparents this summer.*

4 You are going to interview people at a technology fair. Make questions.

1 you and your friends / look at / the new social networking site?
Are you and your friends going to look at the new social networking site?
2 your dad / use / IM?
3 teacher / buy / an interactive whiteboard?
4 you / read / a blog?
5 your mom / replace / her old cell phone with a smart phone?
6 you / watch / a movie on a big screen?

Pronunciation Weak form of *to*

5a Listen to the word *to* in these questions.

3.32 1 Are you going to play on this new game console?
2 Is your dad going to buy a netbook?
3 Is your mom going to ask about broadband?
4 Are you going to listen to this digital radio?

b Listen again and repeat.
3.32

6 In pairs, ask and answer the questions in Exercise 4.

7 What about you? In pairs, talk about three pieces of technology you're going to use this week.

> I'm going to go on Facebook this evening. It's my favorite social networking site.

> I'm going to write a blog on the Internet about my school.

Vocabulary • Technology phrases

1 Complete the technology phrases with these verbs. Then listen, check and repeat.
3.33

> charge   chat   download   ~~go~~   send (x2)   use (x3)   write

Word list page 61
Workbook page 132

Go **online** today—buy a ticket for the technology fair.

You can .... **Wi-Fi** to play the latest games. They're really exciting!

You can .... **the Internet** on a super fast broadband connection.

You can .... **emails** to our technology experts and ask your technology questions.

You can .... **a text** to our technology contest— the prize is a netbook!

You can .... **online** with a sports star, a pop star and an actor! Ask them a question!

You can .... **a blog** about your day—take some photos, too.

You can .... **videos, music and movies**—it's all free today!

You can learn how to .... **a** new **search engine**.

You can .... **your cell phone** with a solar-powered charger—it uses energy from the sun!

2 Choose words from Exercise 1 to complete each sentence.

1 People can send information by *email* or .... .
2 You can download .... , ... or .... from the Internet.
3 You can write a .... .
4 You can chat .... with a pop star.
5 You can use .... , a .... or the .... .
6 You charge your .... with a solar-powered charger.

3 What about you? Imagine you are at a technology fair. Choose some activities to do. Make a list. Tell the class.

Morning   *use Wi-Fi to play games, ...*
Afternoon   *download movies, ...*
Evening   *write ... .*

> In the morning, I'm going to use Wi-Fi to play games.

Brain Trainer Activity 4
Go to page 66

Chatroom Asking for information

Speaking and Listening

1 Look at the photo. Where are Monica, Julia and Nick?

a at the Wildlife Club
b at a radio station
c at school

2 Listen and read the conversation. Are the statements true (T) or false (F)?

3.34

1 The Wildlife Club helped some animals last week. *F*
2 The council wanted to build a road in Willow End.
3 The club sent photos to a newspaper.
4 The council decided not to build at Willow End.
5 There are five people in the club.
6 The club isn't looking for new members.

3 Act out the conversation in groups of four.

DJ	Welcome to Radio X! I'm talking to a Wildlife Club today. Hi, guys! Now, last month your Wildlife Club helped some animals. Can you tell us more?
Julia	Yes. We found rare otters in Willow End, but the city council wanted to build a new neighborhood there.
DJ	What happened?
Nick	We took photos of the otters to the newspaper, and the council isn't building it now.
DJ	That's awesome! Now, tell me about your club.
Monica	Well, it's small—four people … and a dog!
DJ	And what are you planning?
Julia	Well, this summer we're creating a nature reserve for the otters, so we're looking for more members.
DJ	OK, we're helping the club to find more members, so call in now!
Nick	Thank you.

Say it in your language …
That's awesome!
Well, …

4 **Look back at the conversation. Who says what?**

1 Can you tell us more? *DJ*
2 What happened?
3 That's awesome!
4 Tell me about your club.
5 What are you planning?
6 Well, this summer we're creating a nature reserve.

5 **Look back at the conversation again. What phrases does the DJ use to ask about these things?**

1 the club
2 the club's plans for the summer

6 **Read the phrases for asking for information.**

Past	Present	Future
What happened?	Can you tell us more? Tell me about …	What are you planning?

7 **Listen to the conversations. Act out the conversations in pairs.**

3.35

Kenji   I'm not going on vacation this summer.
May   Oh, what are you planning?
Kenji   I'm [1] seeing my friends every day.

Tom   I got a bad grade on my [2] math test.
Olivia   Why? What happened?
Tom   Oh, I didn't understand the instructions.

Zoe   I started an awesome blog last week.
Luke   Really? Tell me about it.
Zoe   Well, it's about [3] social networking sites.

8 **Work in pairs. Replace the words in purple in Exercise 7. Use these words and/or your own ideas. Act out the conversations.**

> What are you planning this summer?

> I'm traveling to the mountains.

1 writing a blog / chatting online / going to the swimming pool

2 English homework / science test / history essay

3 the Internet / downloading music / using a search engine

Grammar • Present continuous for future arrangements

Affirmative		
I	'm (am)	going to a party tonight.
You/We/They	're (are)	
He/She/It	's (is)	

Negative		
I	'm not (am not)	playing basketball tomorrow.
You/We/They	aren't (are not)	
He/She/It	isn't (is not)	

Questions and short answers		
Are	you/we/they	watching a movie tonight?
Is	he/she/it	

Yes, I am. / No, I'm not.

Yes, you/we/they are. / No, you/we/they aren't.

Yes, he/she/it is. / No, he/she/it isn't.

Grammar reference page 126

1 **Study the grammar table.**

2 **Complete the conversations with the Present continuous affirmative or negative.**

A Are *you wearing* (you / wear) dressy clothes to Oscar's party next week?
B No, …. (I / not / go) in dressy clothes.

A I …. (stay / at home) tonight. What about you? Are …. (you / go) out?
B Yes, I am. I …. (help) the Wildlife Club.

A Emma …. (not / come) to school tomorrow.
B Why not?
A Because …. (she / fly) to Los Angeles with her parents.

3 **What are these people doing this week and on the weekend?**

1 You   3 You and your friends
2 Your friend   4 Your teacher

4 **In pairs, ask and answer the questions in Exercise 3.**

> What are you doing this weekend?

> I'm going to a new dance class.

Reading

1 Look at the text. What is it?

a a phone conversation
b an interview
c a chatroom discussion

Technology-Free Week!

Remember, next week is the last week of the school year, and the school is having an official "technology-free" week—so the chatroom is going offline. How are YOU going to live without technology? Tell us your plans for "technology-free" week here!

Comments ▼

Why are you doing this to us? I think it's insane. In fact, it's not possible! I'm going to go crazy! I can't live without my MP3 player. It's going to be soooo difficult. I'm going to sing songs all week.
Skaterboy

Last year I went on vacation to a farm. There wasn't any TV, and we didn't have a computer. I can live without these things, but it isn't fun! I'm going to play a lot of sports next week.
Anya12

I'm going to read ... and eat. In the evenings, my friends and I are going to have parties. We're going to play music on the radio—is that OK? Is that technology?
Madmax

In my opinion, technology is a problem. We sit around all day, and we don't get much exercise. We don't talk. We can't hear because we have earphones in our ears all day. Technology-free week is a great idea! I think it's fun, too. Are you going to film us?
Smiley

Key Words

technology-free	offline	to live without
insane	crazy	earphones

2 Read and check your answer to Exercise 1.

3 Read the text. Are the sentences true (T) or false (F)?
3.36

1 Skaterboy likes the idea of "technology-free" week. *F*
2 Skaterboy is going to study all week.
3 Anya12 thinks life without technology is great.
4 Anya12 is going to go to a farm.
5 Madmax is going to have a lot of parties.
6 Smiley agrees with "technology-free" week.

4 Read the text again. Answer the questions.
3.36

1 What is a technology-free week?
   It's a week where you can't use technology.
2 Is Skaterboy happy with the idea?
3 What is Anya12 going to do?
4 What is Madmax going to play music on?
5 Why does Smiley think that technology is a problem?

Listening

1 Listen to the interview. Which words do you hear?
3.37

chat	download	email	novel
online	search engine	Wi-Fi	

2 Listen again. Answer the questions.
3.37

1 Speaker A is going to …
   a learn to use a computer.
   b work for his dad.
   c help his grandpa.
2 Speaker B is going to …
   a go online every day.
   b teach her friends tennis.
   c go to the beach.
3 Speaker C is going to …
   a write a short story.
   b read a "keitai" novel.
   c write a Twitter novel.

Writing • A story

1 Read the Writing File.

> **Writing File** Review
>
> **Remember to use all your writing skills!**
>
> a **Check your punctuation**
>   Do you have periods, capital letters, commas,
>   question marks and exclamation points?
> b **Use linking words**
>   Use *and*, *but* or *because* to join words,
>   phrases or sentences.
> c **Write in paragraphs**
>   Is the information in a group?

2 Read the story and find more examples of each
writing skill.

The Time Machine
A short story by
Olivia da Silva, age 12

My friend, the Professor, has a Time Machine. It's
amazing, but it's a secret! This evening we're
going to travel to the future. I want to see my town
in 2050!

The Time Machine is small and black. There's a big screen
and a lot of computers. In fact, you can get Wi-Fi and
download videos!

We're traveling very fast now ... BANG! What was that?
We're in another time, but when?
I'm going to open the door ... We're walking out into the
street. People are wearing long white clothes. Oh no!
We aren't in the future. We're in Rome, 2,000 years ago.
It's exciting, but we're going home soon—it's late!

3 Read the story again. Answer the questions.

1 What is Olivia's friend's name? *the Professor*
2 Is the Time Machine big?
3 What can you do in the Time Machine?
4 Do they travel to the past?
5 How many years ago was it?
6 Why is Olivia going home?

4 Choose the correct options to make sentences.

1 Joanna's traveling in time , / . but I'm not.
2 Are you going to fly , / ?
3 They aren't going to the past . / ?
4 I don't have an e-reader, *and* / *but* my dad does.
5 William's using a search engine *but* / *because*
  he's doing his homework.
6 We're going to download music *and* / *but*
  videos this evening.

5 Choose your means of transportation and
your place. Take notes about your journey.

Transportation time machine / space rocket
Place space / the moon / a new planet

6 Write a story. Use "My story" and your notes
from Exercise 5.

> **My story**
>
> **Title**
> Think of a title for your story.
>
> **Paragraph 1**
> Who is your friend?
> Do you want to visit the past or the future?
> What do you want to see there?
>
> **Paragraph 2**
> Describe your time machine or space rocket.
>
> **Paragraph 3**
> Describe the place and things (and people)
> you can see.
>
> What place (and time) are you in?

Remember!
- Use punctuation, linking words
  and paragraphs.
- Use the vocabulary in this unit.
- Check your grammar and spelling.

Refresh Your Memory!

Grammar • Review

1 Complete the text with the correct form of *be going to*.

We ¹ *'re going to go* (go) on vacation to Mexico this summer. We ² .... (take) a lot of things! My mom ³ .... (read) some e-books, and my dad ⁴ .... (send) emails on his smart phone in the evenings. I ⁵ .... (listen) to a lot of new songs on my MP3 player, and my two sisters ⁶ .... (do) their homework on their laptop.

2 Make the questions for the vacation questionnaire.

1 *Are you going to watch TV in your room?*

Vacation questionnaire

		Bella	Jessica	Freddie
1	watch TV in your room?	✗	✓	✗
2	eat pizza every week?	✓	✗	✓
3	go swimming every day?	✓	✓	✗
4	see all your friends?	✓	✓	✓
5	play basketball?	✗	✗	✓
6	do any homework?	✗	✗	✗

3 Make six sentences about the three children in Exercise 2.

1 *Jessica is going to watch TV in her room, but Bella and Freddie aren't going to watch TV in their rooms.*

4 Make sentences about arrangements for tomorrow using the Present continuous.

1 Olivia / get up / 11 a.m.
 Olivia is getting up at 11 a.m.
2 I / study / online in the morning
3 Isabella and Carlos / not go / to the movies
4 My brother / wash / Dad's car
5 Fiona / not clean up / her room
6 We / have / chicken and potatoes for dinner

Vocabulary • Review

5 Match five technology words.

1 *digital radio*

digital	drive	flash	instant
interactive	messaging	networking	radio
site	social	whiteboard	

6 Choose the correct options.

1 How often do you *use / send / go* online?
2 Can you *use / write / read* Wi-Fi at school?
3 We often *charge / use / chat* the Internet for homework.
4 Mom *uses / chats / sends* emails to all her friends at Christmas.
5 Do you *use / charge / send* many texts?
6 I often *chat / send / charge* online with my cousins in Atlanta.
7 I'm going to *read / charge / go* my cell phone before I go on vacation.
8 She doesn't often *chat / use / download* music.

Speaking • Review

7 Match the questions (a–c) to the answers (1–3).
3.38 Then listen and check.

a What are your plans for the summer?
b What happened?
c Can you tell me more?

1 I passed my exam!
2 Yes! We're doing a radio show soon.
3 I'm going to go surfing.

Dictation

8 Listen and write in your notebook.
3.39

✓ **My assessment profile:** page 146

Citizenship File

The Statewide Youth Council of Massachusetts

Eddie and Brianna are ordinary high school students in Massachusetts. But they also have an important job. They are members of the Statewide Youth Council. There are twenty-eight members on the Council, all between 14 and 20 years old. Their job is to represent young people in their city or town for two years.

All young people from Massachusetts can apply to be Council members, and a special committee reads their applications and chooses the best candidates. The members of the Youth Council meet every two months. They talk to the governor of Massachusetts about the problems young people face in their area. Together with the governor, they discuss their ideas and make a plan of action.

The members of the Youth Council work on many different things. For example, between 2012 and 2014, they organized an antibullying campaign in schools. They discussed bullying and possible solutions with students, and helped pass new laws against bullying. They also encouraged other young people to take part in their community. In 2015 the Youth Council is planning to focus on young people's education and health.

Eddie says, "Youth Council means that our opinion is important." Brianna adds, "But the best part is that we help make a difference in the lives of other young people."

Reading

1 Read the text quickly. Why are Eddie and Brianna important people?

2 Read the text again. Answer the questions.

3.40 1 What do Youth Council members do?
They represent young people from their city or town.

2 How many Statewide Youth Council members are there?

3 How old are the Youth Council members?

4 How long do young people work for the Youth Council?

5 What did the Youth Council do between 2012 and 2014?

My Citizenship File

3 You want to be a Youth Council member. Think about your application.

- What are the problems in your area?
- What are your ideas?

4 Write five sentences for your application in your notebook.

Review 3

Grammar • Past simple: *to be*

1 **Change the sentences into the Past simple.**

1 I'm in Mexico. *I was in Mexico.*
2 He isn't a teacher.
3 Are you in the hospital?
4 Is it cold?
5 Am I late?
6 They aren't very big.

• There was/There were

2 **Complete the conversation with the correct form of *there was/there were*.**

A ¹ *Was there* a party on Saturday night?
B Yes, ² .... . It was at Sam's house.
A ³ .... a lot of people at the party?
B No, ⁴ .... . It was small, but it was fun!
A ⁵ .... any good music?
B Yes, the music was awesome. ⁶ .... a lot of dancing, too. Yasmin's dancing was amazing!

• Past simple

3 **Complete the sentences with the Past simple.**

1 I *stopped* (stop) at the station at 7:15 a.m.
2 He .... (study) Japanese in Tokyo for two years. Then he .... (work) for a Japanese bank.
3 I .... (call) Katie on her cell phone this morning, but she .... (not answer).
4 They .... (talk) to their mom about the problem and .... (ask) her for advice.
5 We .... (travel) around Oregon last summer, but we .... (not like) the weather!

4 **Complete the text with the Past simple form of these verbs.**

clean   cook   hate   play   rain   ~~start~~   stay   stop

The rain ¹ *started* at 7 a.m. yesterday, and it ² .... (not). It ³ .... all day. I ⁴ .... (not) soccer because of the weather. I ⁵ .... at home, and my sister and I ⁶ .... up our rooms. Mom ⁷ .... pasta for dinner, but I ⁸ .... the vegetables with it. Yuck! What a terrible day!

5 **What did Brandon do on Saturday? What didn't he do? Make sentences.**

1 *He got up early.*
2 *He didn't have a healthy breakfast.*

• get up early	✓
• have a healthy breakfast	✗
• go to the mall	✓
• buy a present for Cara	✗
• have lunch with Dan	✓
• do his math homework	✓
• give Cara her present	✗

6 **Complete the text with the Past simple.**

"How many seconds are there in a minute?" the teacher ¹ *asked* (ask) when the students ² .... (come) into the classroom. The question ³ .... (not be) difficult. "Sixty," they ⁴ .... (answer). "Good. And how many seconds in a year?" the teacher ⁵ .... (continue). The students ⁶ .... (think) for a moment, but they ⁷ .... (not know). Only Jim ⁸ .... (put) his hand up. "Twelve," he ⁹ .... (say). "There's January 2nd, February 2nd, March 2nd, ..."

7 **Make questions and answers with the Past simple.**

1 when / they / leave / ?   (at six thirty)
   When did they leave?
   They left at six thirty.
2 I / say / the wrong thing / ?   (yes)
3 what / he / give / his mom / ?   (a book)
4 you / understand / the question / ?   (no)
5 how many / glasses of juice / we / drink / ? (nine)
6 they / help / Matt / ?   (yes)

8 **Complete the conversation in the Past simple.**

A Where ¹ *did you go* (go) on vacation this year?
B We ² .... (travel) around Europe by train.
A Cool! How many days ³ .... (the trip, take)?
B It ⁴ .... (take) two weeks.
A ⁵ .... (you, visit) any interesting cities?
B Yes, we ⁶ .... . We ⁷ .... (see) the Eiffel Tower in Paris, and we also ⁸ .... (go) to Vienna, Budapest and Athens.
A ⁹ .... (you, come) home by train?
B No, we ¹⁰ .... . We ¹¹ .... (fly).

• Be going to

9 Make sentences about future plans with *be going to*.

1 I / see a movie / this weekend
I'm going to see a movie this weekend.
2 they / walk / to the park / on Saturday
3 Sally and I / not clean up / our room / tonight
4 a new store / open / in the shopping mall / soon
5 she / not come / with us / tomorrow
6 I / be / a doctor

10 Complete the conversation with the correct form of *be going to*.

A What are your plans for the weekend?
¹ *Are you going to be* (be) at home?
B No, I ² ..... . I ³ .... (visit) my grandparents.
A ⁴ .... (your brothers, go) with you?
B Yes, they ⁵ ..... .
A ⁶ .... (your mom, drive) you there?
B No, she ⁷ ..... . We ⁸ .... (take) the bus.
A ⁹ .... (you, read) a book on the bus?
B Yes, I ¹⁰ .... , but my brothers ¹¹ .... (not do) that. They ¹² .... (play) games on their game consoles.

• Present continuous for future arrangements

11 Read this family's calendar. Make sentences about their plans.

1 *At five o'clock on Monday, Lily's playing tennis with Josh.*

Monday	Lily: 5 p.m., play tennis with Josh
Tuesday	Sam: 6 p.m., see "Tarantula" at the movie theater
Wednesday	Mom: buy food for Dad's birthday dinner Lily and Sam: cook the dinner
Thursday	Lily and Sam: do gymnastics after school
Friday	Mom and Dad: 8 p.m., have dinner at the Red Café Lily: stay at Tasha's house

Speaking • Talking about the past

1 Rewrite the sentences. Use a word or phrase from each box.

ago (x3)	last (x3)	this	yesterday

afternoon	an hour	month	morning
night	~~summer~~	three weeks	twenty minutes

It's now 8 p.m. on Saturday, June 23.

1 They planned the concert in August.
They planned the concert last summer.
2 We heard about it in May.
3 We bought the tickets on June 2.
4 I sent her an email on Friday at 3 p.m.
5 I called her on Friday at 9 p.m.
6 The game started today at 11 a.m.
7 She arrived today at 7 p.m.
8 I saw her today at 7:40 p.m.

• Talking on the phone

2 Put the conversation in the correct order.

Debbie	Hi, Edward. Is the band going to meet tonight?	....
Bill	Hello.	.1.
Debbie	Oh, good. Thanks. See you later!	....
Bill	No, it's Bill.	....
Debbie	Hi. Is this Edward?	.2.
Edward	Bye!	....
Debbie	Oh. Hi, Bill. It's Debbie. Can I speak to Edward, please?	....
Edward	Yes, it is. At six thirty.	....
Bill	OK. Hold on. Here he is.	....

• Asking for information

3 Make questions.

1 you / me / tell / Can / more / ?
2 plans / are / What / your / ?
3 happened / What / ?

Vocabulary • Ordinal numbers, years, dates

1 **Write these dates in full.**

1 Nov. 4, 1989
November fourth, nineteen eighty-nine
2 Jan. 31, 2007   4 Feb. 15, 1995
3 Aug. 22, 2014   5 Mar. 3, 2009

• Regular verbs

2 **Complete the sentences with the correct Past simple form of these verbs.**

answer	ask	call	close	invent	like
listen	stop	study	talk	travel	work

1 I didn't buy any food because the store *closed* early.
2 In 1885 Karl Benz .... the first car. His wife Bertha .... 100 kilometers in it in one day.
3 We .... the Romans in history last week. Jimmy .... some questions about Roman gladiators. Our teacher .... some of his questions, but she didn't know all the answers.
4 Five years ago, my dad .... at a hospital. He .... his job. He was sad when he .... working there.
5 I .... my grandma last night. We .... for a long time, and she .... to all my problems.

• Means of transportation

3 **Complete the sentences with some of these words.**

bike	boat	bus	canoe	car
helicopter	motorcycle	plane	scooter	
subway	train	truck	van	

1 Forty people are going from Madrid to Paris. They can go by *plane* or .... .
2 A family of six needs to travel three kilometers in New York City. But no one has a bike. They can go by .... or .... .
3 You are taking 200 kilos of apples to different stores in the city. You can use a .... or a .... .
4 You want to travel on water. You can use a .... or a .... .

• Clothes

4 **Put these clothes into the correct categories.**

boots	coat	dress	hat	jeans
pants	pajamas	sandals	scarf	shoes
shorts	skirt	sneakers	sweater	T-shirt

on your feet	in bed	on your legs	for cold weather	other
sneakers, ...				

• Technology

5 **Complete the words with the missing letters.**

1 I often do my homework on my n e t b o o k.
2 I like reading novels on my e-r _ _ d _ r.
3 We're listening to our d _ _ it _ _   r _ _ _ o.
4 What's on that f _ _ _ h dr_ _ _?
5 He writes an interesting b _ _ _ about his life.
6 He has b _ _ _ db _ _ d but no W _-F _.
7 We have an int _ _ ac _ _ _ _ w _ _ t _ b _ _ _ d in our classroom.
8 Your computer has a big s _ _ _ _ n!
9 She often goes on s _ c _ _ l n _ _ w _ _ k _ _ _ s _ t _ s, but she never uses i _ _ t _ _ t m _ _ s _ _ _ _ g.

6 **Complete the text with these words.**

chat	charge	download	get	go
read	send	use	write	

I love technology. I [1] *download* a lot of music and videos, and I often [2] .... search engines for my homework. My life is very boring, so I don't [3] .... a blog about it. But my sister is traveling in Asia, and I [4] .... her blog every day. My friends and I often [5] .... online after school, about teachers, homework, everything! I [6] .... my cell phone every night, so it always has power for the next day. I can't [7] .... online with it because it isn't a smart phone. But I [8] .... a lot of texts to my friends, and I [9] .... a lot of texts from them, too.

Word list

Unit 7 • Modern History

Ordinal numbers, years, dates

fifth	/fɪfθ/
first	/fɚst/
fourth	/fɔrθ/
second	/ˈsɛkənd/
third	/θɚd/
thirty-first	/ˈθɚt̬i fɚst/
twentieth	/ˈtwɛntiɪθ/
twenty-second	/ˈtwɛnti ˈsɛkənd/
nineteen fifty-seven	/ˌnaɪnˈtin ˈfɪfti ˈsɛvən/
nineteen forty-two	/ˌnaɪnˈtin ˈfɔrt̬i ˈtu/
nineteen ninety	/ˌnaɪnˈtin ˈnaɪnti/
nineteen twelve	/ˌnaɪnˈtin ˈtwɛlv/
nineteen twenty-two	/ˌnaɪnˈtin twɛnti ˈtu/
twenty eleven	/ˈtwɛnti ɪˈlɛvən/
two thousand	/ˈtu ˈθaʊzənd/
two thousand four	/ˈtu ˈθaʊzənd ənd ˈfɔr/

Regular verbs

answer	/ˈænsɚ/	answered	/ˈænsɚd/
ask	/æsk/	asked	/ˈæskt/
call	/kɔl/	called	/kɔld/
close	/kloʊz/	closed	/kloʊzd/
invent	/ɪnˈvɛnt/	invented	/ɪnˈvɛntɪd/
like	/laɪk/	liked	/ˈlaɪkt/
listen	/ˈlɪsən/	listened	/ˈlɪsənd/
stop	/stɑp/	stopped	/stɑpt/
study	/ˈstʌdi/	studied	/ˈstʌdɪd/
talk	/tɔk/	talked	/tɔkt/
travel	/ˈtrævəl/	traveled	/ˈtrævəld/
work	/wɚk/	worked	/wɚkt/

Unit 8 • Travel

Means of transportation

bike	/baɪk/
boat	/boʊt/
bus	/bʌs/
canoe	/kəˈnu/
car	/kɑr/
helicopter	/ˈhɛləˌkɑptɚ/
motorcycle	/ˈmoʊt̬ɚˌsaɪkəl/
plane	/pleɪn/
scooter	/ˈskut̬ɚ/
subway	/ˈsʌbweɪ/
train	/treɪn/
truck	/trʌk/
van	/væn/

Clothes

boots	/buts/
coat	/koʊt/
dress	/drɛs/
hat	/hæt/
jeans	/dʒinz/
pajamas	/pəˈdʒɑməz, -ˈdʒæ-/
pants	/pænts/
sandals	/ˈsændəlz/
scarf	/skɑrf/
shoes	/ʃuz/
shorts	/ʃɔrts/
skirt	/skɚt/
sneakers	/ˈsnikɚz/
sweater	/ˈswɛt̬ɚ/
T-shirt	/ˈti ʃɚt/

Unit 9 • Technology Time

Technology

blog	/blɑg/
broadband	/ˈbrɔdbænd/
digital radio	/ˈdɪdʒɪtl ˈreɪdiˌoʊ/
e-reader	/ˈiˌridɚ/
flash drive	/ˈflæʃ draɪv/
IM (instant messaging)	/aɪ em, ˈɪnstənt ˈmɛsɪdʒɪŋ/
interactive whiteboard	/ˌɪntəˈræktɪv ˈwaɪtbɔrd/
netbook	/ˈnɛtbʊk/
screen	/skrin/
smart phone	/ˈsmɑrt foʊn/
social networking site	/ˈsoʊʃəl ˈnɛtwɚkɪŋ saɪt/
Wi-Fi	/ˈwaɪfaɪ/

Technology phrases

charge your cell phone	/tʃɑrdʒ yɚ ˈsɛl foʊn/
chat online	/tʃæt ˌɑnˈlaɪn/
download movies	/ˌdaʊnloʊd ˈmuviz/
download music	/ˌdaʊnloʊd ˈmyuzɪk/
download videos	/ˌdaʊnloʊd ˈvɪdioʊz/
go online	/goʊ ˈɑnlaɪn/
send a text	/sɛnd ə ˈtɛkst/
send an email	/sɛnd ən ˈimeɪl/
use a search engine	/yuz ə sɚtʃ ˈɛndʒɪn/
use the Internet	/yuz ði ˈɪntɚˌnɛt/
use Wi-Fi	/yuz ˈwaɪfaɪ/
write a blog	/raɪt ə blɑg/

Brain Trainer

Find the difference

1. Look at the photo on page 8 for one minute. Now study this photo. What differences can you find?

Grammar

2. Look at the picture for two minutes. Cover the picture. Now say a square. Your partner says what the person is doing.

   1a – He's climbing.

Vocabulary

3. Look at the picture and find eight activities. You have two minutes!

4. Read the words in each box aloud three times. Cover the words and write them in your notebook. Can you remember all the words?

| hot
sunny | warm
cloudy
windy | cold
foggy
raining
snowing |

Brain Trainer

Find the difference

1 Look at the photo on page 18 for one minute. Now study this photo. What differences can you find?

Grammar

2 Work in pairs. Take turns asking questions and giving answers.

1 *How many* bananas do you have?   four
2 .... pasta do we have?   a lot
3 .... eggs do you have?   (not) any
4 .... juice do you have?   (not) much
5 .... cheese do we have?   some
6 .... ham sandwiches do you have?   two
7 .... tomatoes do you have?   a lot
8 .... bread do we have?   (not) much

How much juice do you have?

I don't have much juice.

Vocabulary

3 How many food words can you make using these letters? You have three minutes!

banana, ...

4 Put the letters in the correct order to make adjectives. You have two minutes!

1 *clean*

1 l e c n a
2 t h o
3 e l r g a
4 d c l o
5 c u s i o i d e l
6 y s n o i
7 t q u e i
8 i n g d i s u g s t
9 d r i y t
10 l l s a m
11 b h o i r r e l
12 f u l e r d n o w

Brain Trainer 7

Find the difference

1 Look at the photo on page 32 for one minute. Now study this photo. What differences can you find?

Grammar

2 Make sentences with words of the same color. Then make your own color puzzle. In pairs, complete your partner's puzzle.

1 *She was at the hospital this morning.*

She	any	morning	classroom	at
the	was	the	station	computers
weren't	wasn't	friends	the	hospital
the	I	There	were	brother
ago	in	Lucy's	My	café
fifteen	at	on	in	They
at	the	this	last	minutes
was	were	ago	TV	the
train	an	week	hour	library

Vocabulary

3a Work in pairs. Choose list A or B. Your partner says the dates. Write them down in your notebook. Switch roles. Then check your answers.

A	B
1904	1931
1956	1989
2008	2003
2014	2012

3b Now try again.

A	B
5/17/1833	12/1/1899
1/29/1990	2/7/1954
4/10/2000	10/20/2007
6/6/2015	8/31/2020

4a Read the words in the box for one minute. Cover the words and write them in your notebook. How many can you remember?

asked	liked	talked
closed	called	worked

4b Now try again.

answered	listened	studied
invented	stopped	traveled

Brain Trainer

Find the difference

1 Look at the photos on page 42 for one minute. Now study these photos. What differences can you find?

Grammar

2 Make sentences with words of the same color. Then make your own color puzzle. In pairs, complete your partner's puzzle.

1 *I went to London yesterday.*

I	took	a	dinner	yesterday
didn't	bought	went	I	new
to	I	a	I	had
the	London	yesterday	sweater	drink
for	buy	train	pizza	I

3 Work in small groups. Act out something you did last weekend. Your classmates guess what you did. The person who gives the correct answer acts out the next activity.

Did you play soccer?

No, I didn't.

Vocabulary

4a Find two transportation words hidden in the grid.

m	o	t	o
c	a	r	r
r	u	l	c
e	l	c	y

4b Now make your own grid. Can your partner find the words?

5a Look at the pictures. What are these items? You have three minutes!

1 *T-shirt*

5b Can you think of five more clothes words? You wear them on your head or your feet.

Brain Trainer

Find the difference

1 Look at the photo on page 52 for one minute. Now study this photo. What differences can you find?

Grammar

2 Look at the picture for two minutes, then cover it. Now say a square. Your partner says what the people are or aren't going to do tomorrow.

3a – They aren't going to visit the museum tomorrow.

Vocabulary

3 Match ten technology words.

1 *interactive whiteboard*

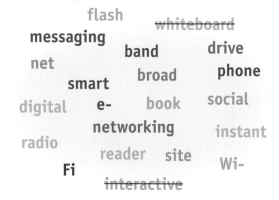

flash ~~whiteboard~~
messaging band drive
net broad phone
smart
digital e- book social
networking
radio instant
reader site Wi-
Fi ~~interactive~~

4 Look at the pictures. What are the mystery phrases?

1 *send an email*

 an

 your

 music

 use the @

 a

 online

 a

Reading

1 **Read the text quickly and look at the photos.**
3.44 **Match the headings (1–5) to each paragraph (A–E).**

1 Water transportation
2 Taxis
3 Biking and walking
4 Buses
5 Subway

2 **Read the text again. Answer the questions.**
3.44
1 Why do a lot of people use public transportation in New York?
2 How many subway stations are there?
3 What two things can you see from the Staten Island Ferry?
4 How many people travel by bike every day?
5 What do you use to pay your fare on a bus?
6 What color are New York City cabs?

Your culture

3 **In pairs, answer the questions.**

1 What are the main means of transportation in your major cities?
2 How do students get to your school?
3 Write a short paragraph to describe one of the means of transportation in your capital city.

New York

is a very populous city, and there are a lot of ways to travel around it. Traveling by car is expensive and often slow because of traffic, so many people use public transportation.

A ...
There are 468 subway stations and 24 different lines. New York has one of the largest subway systems in the world.

B ...
Manhattan is an island. Over 19 million people a year take the Staten Island Ferry. Some take it to go to work, and other passengers are tourists. From the boat, you can see the Statue of Liberty and the lower Manhattan skyline.

C ...
Over 200,000 city residents travel by bike every day. In fact, biking and walking together make up 21% of all trips in New York City.

D ...
More than 2 million people travel on the New York City buses every day. Over 5,900 buses run on over 200 local and express routes in the city. Passengers on a bus can use the same fare card that they use on the subway. There are also special yellow buses that take New York children to school.

E ...
New York City taxis, or cabs, are known for their distinctive yellow color. Over 13,000 taxis operate in the city. The taxi drivers know every street in New York City. It's a very hard job!

Reading

1 Read the text quickly. Complete each paragraph
3.45 with the correct information.

a Rock'n'Roll
b swim fins and eyeglasses
c about 1,800 poems
d Civil Rights Movement

2 Read the text again. Are these statements
3.45 true (T) or false (F)?

1 The United States declared independence
from France.
2 Emily Dickinson published her poems
in magazines.
3 Elvis is often called the Prince.
4 Martin Luther King Jr. was a leader of
the African-American community.

Your culture

3 In pairs, do these activities.

1 Write the names of five famous people from
your country and say why they are famous.
• a writer
• a sports star
• a painter
• an actor
• a scientist
2 Write a short paragraph about one
of the famous people from your country.
Include this information:
• Date of birth
• Where does (did) he/she live?
• What does (did) he/she do?
• Why is (was) he/she famous?

■ Benjamin Franklin (1706–1790) ■

Benjamin Franklin is best known as one of the politicians
who signed the American Declaration of Independence
from Great Britain. However, he was also an author,
a printer, a scientist, a diplomat and an inventor. We still
use some of Franklin's inventions, such as [1] ..... .

■ Emily Dickinson (1830–1886)■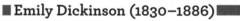

Emily Dickinson was a poet. She lived a quiet and private
life, and she never got married or had children. She wrote
[2] ...., but she only shared some of them with her family
and friends. When Dickinson died, her family decided to
publish her poetry. Now Emily Dickinson is considered one
of the greatest American poets.

■ Elvis Presley (1935–1977)■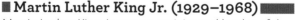

Elvis Presley was an American singer and actor.
He is often called the King of [3] ...., or simply the King.
He sold 600 million of his albums around the world.
He died almost 40 years ago, but his music still inspires
artists today.

■ Martin Luther King Jr. (1929–1968)■

Martin Luther King Jr. was an activist and leader of the
African-American [4] ..... He organized peaceful protests
and demonstrations against racism and discrimination
directed at African Americans. In 1964 he received the
Nobel Peace Prize for his work. Four years later, he was
assassinated in Memphis, Tennessee.

Reading

1 Read the text quickly and match the photos (A–D)
3.46 to each festival or holiday.

2 Read the text again. Answer the questions.
3.46
  1 What do people give each other on
    Valentine's Day?
  2 What happens in some cities and towns
    on the Fourth of July?
  3 Why do American children enjoy Halloween?
  4 Who do Americans remember on Thanksgiving?

3 In pairs, do these activities.
  1 Write a list of festivals and celebrations
    from your country.
  2 Describe a special festival or celebration.
    Include this information:
    • When is it?
    • Where is it?
    • Do you eat special food?
    • How do you celebrate it?

Valentine's Day

Valentine's Day falls on February 14. It's a popular holiday
in the US, celebrating love and friendship. People give
each other cards and small gifts, such as chocolates,
flowers or teddy bears, to show their love, friendship
or respect. Some people also organize Valentine's Day
parties or dinners with their friends or family.

Independence Day

This public holiday is also known as the Fourth of July.
It celebrates the day the United States adopted the
Declaration of Independence. Some cities and towns
organize Fourth of July parades and fireworks displays.
Many people also spend this holiday with their families
and have a barbecue or a picnic.

Halloween

Halloween is celebrated on October 31. It's a popular
holiday among children, who put on scary or funny
costumes and visit their neighbors, asking them for candy.
Teenagers and adults sometimes wear costumes too,
but they usually celebrate Halloween by going to parties
or by watching scary movies.

Thanksgiving

Thanksgiving falls on the fourth Thursday of November.
On that day, Americans remember the early settlers—the
Pilgrims—who held a big celebration to thank God for a good
harvest. Most families have a special dinner and serve some of
the foods that the Pilgrims had at their feast. The most popular
Thanksgiving dishes are roast turkey with cranberry sauce and
sweet potatoes, along with cornbread and pumpkin pie.

MOVE IT!

WORKBOOK WITH MP3S

SPLIT EDITION

1B

CHARLOTTE COVILL

SERIES CONSULTANT: CARA NORRIS-RAMIREZ

Contents

Out and About!

Vocabulary • Activities

★ 1 Circle the complete names of the activities.

bowling	climbing	dancing
the flute	gymnastics	hiking
horseback	ice	kayaking
mountain	(painting)	rollerblading
singing	surfing	

★ 2 Write the activities from Exercise 1 under the correct pictures.

1 *painting* 2 .... 3 ....

4 .... 5 .... 6 ....

7 .... 8 .... 9 ....

★ 3 Complete the phrases with the rest of the words in Exercise 1. Then number the pictures.

1 *ice* skating 3 playing ....
2 .... riding 4 .... biking

a ☐   b ☐

c ☐   d ☐

★★ 4 Complete the sentences.

1 I hate [+ *an activity you do outside*]

....

2 I don't like [+ *an activity you do at home*]

....

3 I like [+ *an activity you do on the weekend*]

....

4 I love [+ *a sport*] ....

★ 5 Complete the sentences with these activities.

bowling	dancing
horseback riding	ice skating
kayaking	~~mountain biking~~
painting	play an instrument

1 She has a bike, and she goes *mountain biking* every week.
2 He goes .... with his horse in the summer.
3 Do you like .... in the ocean?
4 We often go to clubs because we like

....
5 I sometimes go .... on the ice in the winter.
6 I don't like art because I don't like

....
7 You need a large, heavy ball for

....
8 In music class we can ....

★★★ 6 Choose an activity and write your own short description. Use the models in Exercise 5.

Activity	Equipment	Place
surfing	surfboard	in the ocean
dancing	dancing shoes	in a theater
horseback riding	horse	in the mountains
painting	paint and paper	in the countryside

Workbook page 128

Reading

★ 1 Read the extract from a story. Match the people (1–5) to the activities (a–e).

1 Ross and Lizzy   a mountain biking
2 The birds   b hiking
3 A girl   c having a picnic
4 A man   d horseback riding
5 A family   e singing

Brain Trainer

Put new words in topic groups. This will help you learn them more easily and understand texts about a particular topic.

Look at the words and guess which word is not in the story.

adventure	horseback riding	mountains
hiking	river	swims
climb	bike	

Now read the text and check.

Ross and Lizzy are at an adventure camp. It's the first day of their vacation, and they are horseback riding in the mountains. It's a beautiful afternoon. The sun is shining, and the birds are singing. The horses aren't walking very fast. They can see some people. A girl is mountain biking, there's a man hiking with his dog, and a family is having a picnic next to the river. Suddenly, there's a loud noise. Someone is shouting for help. Ross and Lizzy get down from their horses and run to the river.

"Look! There's a boy in the water. He can't swim," says Lizzy.

Ross jumps into the river and swims to him.

Ross says to the boy, "It's OK. I can help you."

Ross and the boy climb out of the water onto the grass. The boy is safe, but he's crying.

"What's wrong?" asks Ross.

"My bike's in the river with my cell phone and keys."

The children look at the water.

"There it is," says the boy.

"What's that next to your bike?" asks Lizzy. "It isn't moving, and it's big. What is it?"

★ 2 Read the extract again. Are the statements true (T) or false (F)?

1 Ross and Lizzy are on vacation.   *T*
2 The man has a dog with him.   ....
3 The horses run to the river.   ....
4 There's a girl in the water.   ....
5 Ross doesn't help the boy.   ....
6 The boy's bike is in the river.   ....

★ 3 Read the extract again. Choose the correct options.

1 Ross and Lizzy (are) / *aren't* in the mountains.
2 The family *has* / *doesn't have* a dog.
3 Ross and Lizzy *hear* / *don't hear* a loud noise.
4 The boy *can* / *can't* swim.
5 Ross *jumps* / *doesn't jump* into the river.

★★★ 4 Guess what's in the river next to the boy's bike. Then read and find out what it is.

1 a fish
2 a box full of money
3 an old statue
4 an old boat

"Look, Lizzy. It's the head of an old statue— the head of the statue in the town square."

"Why is it here?"

"I don't know. Let's call the adventure camp and tell them. They can help us get the bike out of the river, too."

Grammar • Present continuous

★① **Look at the picture. Complete the sentences with the Present continuous affirmative of these verbs.**

| play | ~~rollerblade~~ | run | sing | walk | watch |

1 The girl *'s rollerblading* in the park.
2 The boy ....
3 The children .... in the playground.
4 Their grandparents .... them.
5 The woman .... with her dog.
6 The bird .... in the tree.

★② **Complete the sentences with the Present continuous negative of these verbs.**

| dance | ~~have~~ | run | take |

At the camp …
1 The children *aren't having* lunch outside because the weather is bad.
2 He .... in the race because he can't find his sneakers.
3 They .... because there isn't any music.
4 I .... photos today because I don't have my camera.

★★③ **Look at the pictures. Write sentences.**

1 hike / bike
  They *aren't hiking. They're biking.*
2 swim / surf
  The man ....
3 dance / do gymnastics
  My sister ....
4 take photos / paint
  The children ....

★★④ **Complete the text with the correct form of the verbs.**

The camp is busy today. We [1] *'re doing* (do) a lot of different activities. Some people [2] .... (swim) in the lake. I [3] .... (not swim) because it's cold. I [4] .... (kayak) with Will and Beth. Our counselor, Mr. Carter, [5] .... (check) the boats, and he [6] .... (tell) us what to do. My brother and sister are in the mountains. They [7] .... (go) up Mount Peak today. They [8] .... (not walk); they [9] .... (bike) to the top.

• Present continuous: questions and short answers

★⑤ **Complete the questions with *Am, Is* or *Are*.**

1 *Are* you painting those flowers?
2 .... I playing tennis with you?
3 .... the cat climbing the tree?
4 .... Ben and Emma surfing?
5 .... the girl ice skating?

★⑥ **Match the questions in Exercise 5 to the answers (a–e).**

a No, it isn't.   ☐   d Yes, you are.   ☐
b No, I'm not.   [1]   e Yes, they are.   ☐
c Yes, she is.   ☐

★★⑦ **Look at the pictures. Complete the questions and answers.**

1 *Is he skateboarding?*   (skateboard)
  No, he isn't.
2 .... ?   (surf)
  ....
3 .... ?   (bowl)
  ....
4 .... ?   (run)
  ....

Grammar Reference pages 118–119

Vocabulary • Weather and seasons

★ 1 Find the seasons. Then complete the sentences.

summerwarmspringhotautumncoldwinter

1 The days are hot and sunny, and people go to the beach in *summer*.
2 It often snows in ....
3 In .... the plants grow, and the trees are in flower.
4 It's foggy and windy in .... , and the leaves on the trees turn brown.

★ 2 Find and write the other words in Exercise 1.

1 .... 2 .... 3 ....

★ 3 Label the weather symbols.

| cloudy | ~~foggy~~ | raining |
| snowing | sunny | windy |

1 *foggy*

2 ....

3 .... 4 ....

5 .... 6 ....

★★ 4 Look at the pictures. Write the season and weather.

1 *It's winter. It's cold, and it's snowing.*

2 ....

3 ....

4 ....

★★ 5 Complete the sentences with your own ideas.

1 In the fall the weather *is / isn't*
....

2 In summer I *go / don't go* to
....

3 I *like / don't like* winter because
....

4 In spring we *can / can't* (see)
....

5 My favorite season is
....
because ....

Workbook page 128

Speaking and Listening

★ **(1)** **Listen and complete the table.**
18

Expresses surprise	Doesn't express surprise
1	

★ **(2)** **Listen and read the conversation. Who is surprised,**
19 **Frank or Beth? Underline the expressions of surprise.**

Beth Hi, Frank. I'm glad you're here. Do you have your camera with you?

Frank I have my cell phone. I can take photos with that. Why do you need a camera?

Beth Can you see those two people over there? They're playing tennis.

Frank Yes. Who are they?

Beth That's Brad Pitt and Anthony Mackie.

Frank Wow! How amazing! Why are they here?

Beth They're filming in a big house downtown.

Frank Really? That's cool.

Beth Let's take some photos.

Frank And look! There's Angelina Jolie as well! She's my favorite actor.

Beth We can ask for their autographs, too. This is so exciting!

Speaking and Listening page 133

★★ **(3)** **Read the conversation in Exercise 2 again. Complete the sentences.**

1 Beth asks Frank for a *camera*.
2 Frank has his .... with him.
3 Brad Pitt and Anthony Mackie are playing
....
4 Angelina Jolie is Frank's favorite
....
5 Frank and Beth want the actors' photos
and ....

★★ **(4)** **Complete the conversations with these responses.**

> How amazing! Can you talk to him?
> Look! There's a man juggling six balls!
> ~~Really? That's a lot of babies!~~
> Wow! That's awesome! Thank you so much.

1 Flies can have five trillion babies in one year!
Really? That's a lot of babies!
2 Guess what? I'm standing next to Leo Messi!
....
3 This is a great festival.
....
4 I have a surprise for you. Here are some tickets to Disneyland.
....

★★ **(5)** **Complete the conversation with your ideas.**
★

You	Hi, ¹ .... (name) How are you?
Your friend	I'm fine, thanks. Where are you?
You	I'm in ² .... (place)
Your friend	³ .... (response). What are you doing there?
You	I'm on vacation with ⁴ .... (friend or family member). We're ⁵ .... (activity)
Your friend	⁶ .... (response) Guess what I'm doing!
You	Are you ⁷ .... (activity)?
Your friend	No, I'm in ⁸ .... (place), and I'm talking to ⁹ .... (person)
You	¹⁰ .... (response)

Grammar • Present simple and Present continuous

★ (1) **Match each person to two sentences.**

1 [c] [f]  student

2 [ ] [ ]  doctor

3 [ ] [ ]  artist

4 [ ] [ ]  radio DJ

5 [ ] [ ]  actor

6 [ ] [ ]  zookeeper

a I work in the hospital.
b I'm interviewing Katy Perry for today's show.
c I'm doing my homework now.
d I usually work in the theater.
e I paint pictures of people.
f I walk to school every morning.
g I'm making a movie in Hollywood at the moment.
h I always get up early to feed the animals.
i I'm cleaning out the animal enclosures now.
j I play songs on the radio every morning.
k I'm taking care of a sick baby.
l I'm drawing a girl at the moment.

★ (2) **Write the sentences in Exercise 1 in the correct place.**

1 Present simple: What do they usually do?
  1 *I walk to school every morning.*
  2 ....
  3 ....
  4 ....
  5 ....
  6 ....

2 Present continuous: What are they doing now?
  1 *I'm doing my homework now.*
  2 ....
  3 ....
  4 ....
  5 ....
  6 ....

Grammar Reference pages 118–119

★★ (3) **Complete the description with the Present simple or Present continuous form of the verbs.**

Ms. Sutton [1] *is* (be) a PE teacher. She
[2] .... (work) at the middle school
in Purcell. Every day she [3] ....
(get up) early and [4] ....
(bike) to school. Classes [5] ....
(start) at 9 a.m. Today is Wednesday,
and at the moment she [6] ....
(teach) the first class. The students
[7] .... (not play) soccer outside
because it [8] .... (rain). They
[9] .... (do) gymnastics indoors.

> **Brain Trainer**
>
> **Look for patterns in the language. Is the word order for questions the same in the Present simple and the Present continuous?**
>
> | Auxiliary verb | Subject | Main verb |
> | --- | --- | --- |
> | *Are* | *you* | *studying English now?* |
> | *Do* | *you* | *have any pets?* |
>
> **Now do Exercise 4.**

★★★ (4) **Write the questions and true answers.**

1 you / study English / now?
  Are you studying English now?   Yes, I am.
2 it / rain / at the moment?
  ....
  ....
3 you / sometimes / get up early?
  ....
  ....
4 your family / usually / watch TV / in the evening?
  ....
  ....
5 you / go to the movies / on the weekend?
  ....
  ....
6 your teacher / give you homework / every week?
  ....
  ....

Reading

1 Read Holly's diary. Write the days under the correct weather.

1 ....

2 *Monday*

3 ....

4 ....

5 ....

Holly

Monday
My brothers and I are visiting my grandparents this week. They live in a small house in the country. They have some chickens and a pet goat. I love it here, but we can't see very much at the moment because it's foggy!

Tuesday
We get up early every day because there's a lot to do. In the mornings, Grandpa feeds the animals and cleans the enclosures. We help him. Today we're helping him in the yard. He's making a shed, but it isn't a good day to do this because it's very windy!

Wednesday
We're hiking today. It's cloudy, but it isn't cold. It's very good weather for walking! At the moment we're eating our lunch next to a lake. Grandma makes fantastic picnics!

Thursday
It's hot and sunny, and we're at the beach today. I'm sitting with Grandpa, and we're watching my brothers. They're surfing. It's difficult, and they aren't very good!

Friday
We're going home today, and Mom's coming to pick us up. We're waiting for her. It's raining, so we're watching TV.

2 Read Holly's diary again. Complete the sentences with the correct names.

Grandpa	Grandma	Her brothers
~~Holly~~	Mom	

1 *Holly* and her brothers are visiting their grandparents.
2 .... feeds the chickens and the goat every morning.
3 .... makes fantastic picnics.
4 .... can't surf very well.
5 .... is picking up Holly and her brothers.

3 Answer the questions.

1 What animals do Holly's grandparents have?
They have some chickens and a pet goat.
2 What is Grandpa making in the yard?
....
3 Do they get up early every day?
....
4 Where are they having lunch on Wednesday?
....
5 Who's sitting on the beach on Thursday?
....
6 Why are Holly and her brothers watching TV on Friday?
....

Listening

1 Listen and mark Julia and Dan's next subject.
20

1 English ☐   2 art ☐   3 PE ☐   4 science ☐

2 Listen again. Are the statements true (T) or false (F)?
20

1 Helen and George are playing tennis.   *T*
2 Julia and Dan can play golf or tennis.   ....
3 Julia doesn't have her swimsuit with her.   ....
4 Dan likes playing soccer in the rain.   ....
5 Julia goes ice skating every day in winter.   ....
6 Dan's favorite sport is surfing.   ....

Writing • A blog

1 **Put the words in the correct order.**

1 his blog / Paul / writing / is
Paul is writing his blog.
2 start / at one thirty / The races
....
3 doesn't / Newton / the team competition /
win / usually
....
4 is / Paul / a red shirt / wearing / not
....
5 He / in the 100-meter race / is
....

2 **Read the blog. Are the statements in Exercise 1 true (T) or false (F)?**

1 *T*   2 ....   3 ....   4 ....   5 ....

Thursday lunchtime

I'm really excited because it's Sports Day at school today. It's one thirty now, and the races start at two o'clock. At the moment, it's cloudy. This is good because it isn't very hot. There are six different teams. My team is called Newton, and our team color is yellow. The Watt team usually wins the team competition, but this year we want to win. I love running, and I'm in the 400-meter race. I'm also doing the high jump. My mom's coming to watch.

3 **Read the blog again. Complete the chart for Paul.**

	Paul	You
1 What day and time is Sports Day?	*Thursday 2 p.m.*	
2 What's the weather like?		
3 How many teams are there?		
4 What's your team?		
5 What do you wear?		
6 What events are you in?		

4 **Complete the chart in Exercise 3 for you.**

5 **Write a short blog about Sports Day at your school. Use the model in Exercise 2 and your notes from Exercise 4.**

....
....
....
....
....
....
....
....
....
....
....
....
....
....
....
....

6 Delicious!

Vocabulary • Food and drinks

★ **(1)** **Match the descriptions (1–6) to the food (a–f).**

1 I'm having a tuna sandwich and some juice. I have a banana, too.   *e*
2 I have a ham, cheese and tomato sandwich, and a glass of water.   ....
3 I'm eating rice with shrimp, and a yogurt.   ....
4 I want chicken with pasta and broccoli.   ....
5 I'm having fried sausage, eggs and bread.   ....
6 I want salmon, vegetables and a cup of tea.   ....

a Jake   b Florence   c Michael

d Anita   e Sally   f Nick

★ **(2)** **Look at the pictures in Exercise 1. Complete the sentences with these words.**

banana	bread	broccoli
ham, cheese and tomato sandwich		chicken
eggs	juice	pasta
~~rice~~	salmon	sausage
~~shrimp~~	tea	tuna sandwich
vegetables	water	~~yogurt~~

1 Jake is having *rice*, *shrimp* and a *yogurt*.
2 Florence is having .... , ... and ....
3 Michael is having .... , ... and ....
4 Anita is having .... , ... and ....
5 Sally is having a .... , a .... and some ....
6 Nick is having a .... and a glass of ....

★★ **(3)** **Match the sentence beginnings (1–6) to the endings (a–f).**

1 Bread and pasta are *e*
2 Chicken and sausage are
3 Salmon and tuna are
4 Tea and orange juice are
5 Bananas and carrots are
6 Cheese and yogurt are

a fruits and vegetables.
b fish.
c dairy products.
d meat.
e carbohydrates.
f drinks.

★★ **(4)** **Complete the text with these words.**

broccoli	carbohydrates	meat	pasta
salmon	~~vegetables~~	water	yogurt

Every day we eat a lot of different kinds of food. It's good to eat a lot of fruits and [1] *vegetables* like apples and [2] .... because they are healthy foods. Milk, cheese and [3] .... help your bones grow. It is important to eat some [4] .... (like chicken), but don't eat a lot of red meat. It is also good to eat a lot of fish (like [5] ....). We need [6] .... , so eat some bread, [7] .... or rice with every meal. And don't forget to drink a lot of [8] ....

★★ **(5)** **Write five true sentences about your meals.**
★

1 For breakfast, I eat ....
2 For lunch, I usually have ....
3 For dinner, my family ....
4 My favorite food ....
5 My favorite drink ....
6 I don't like ....

Workbook page 129

Reading

★ 1 Read the article quickly. Write where the breakfasts come from.

China ....

cereal

....

★ 2 Read the article again. Write *Emily*, *Aga* or *Ming*.

1 *Aga*'s eating bread.
2 .... 's eating potatoes.
3 .... 's eating rice.
4 .... 's eating carrots.
5 .... 's eating ham.
6 .... 's eating bacon.

★★ 3 Read the article again. Correct the sentences.

1 Emily has a traditional breakfast every day.
   Emily has a traditional breakfast on Sundays.
2 On school days, Emily drinks a glass of orange juice.
   ....
3 Aga never has sausage for breakfast.
   ....
4 Aga's drinking a cup of tea today.
   ....
5 Ming never has a cooked breakfast.
   ....
6 Ming's favorite breakfast is rice with chicken.
   ....

★★★ 4 Answer the questions.

1 What day does Emily say it is?
   She says it's Sunday.
2 Where are the potatoes?
   ....
3 Where can Emily buy more bread?
   ....
4 Where does Aga come from?
   ....
5 Who sometimes cooks breakfast for Aga?
   ....
6 What does Ming usually eat for breakfast?
   ....
7 Who is eating eggs today?
   ....

Breakfast Around the World

The first meal of the day is breakfast. Everyone eats breakfast, but people eat different food in different countries.

My name's Emily, and I'm American. It's Sunday, and we're having a traditional breakfast today. We have some bacon, eggs and cooked potatoes in the fridge. We don't have much bread for toast, but I can buy some more at the supermarket. We don't have a cooked breakfast every day. On school days, I have cereal and a glass of milk.

I'm Aga, and I come from Poland. My mom sometimes cooks me sausage for breakfast, but I usually have bread with some meat or cheese. Today I'm eating bread and ham because we don't have any cheese. I'm drinking a glass of orange juice, too.

My name's Ming, and I'm from China. My breakfast is always cooked. I usually have rice with fish or meat, and vegetables. My favorite breakfast is rice with shrimp, but we don't have any shrimp today. There isn't any chicken, either. There are a lot of vegetables, so I'm having rice with eggs, carrots and broccoli for breakfast this morning.

Grammar • Countable and uncountable nouns

★ **1** Write C (countable) or U (uncountable) next to each word.

1 tea	*U*	4 ham	....
2 potato	....	5 egg	....
3 bread	....	6 juice	....

★ **2** Find the uncountable noun in each group.

1 eggs   (water)   tomatoes   vegetables
2 rice   bananas   sandwiches   potatoes
3 apple   orange   banana   pasta
4 music   song   guitar   MP3 player
5 comic   wallet   money   watch

★★ **3** How do you say these words? Write the words in the correct column. Then listen and check.
21

banana	pasta	potato	salmon
sausage	water	yogurt	

1 chicken	2 to**ma**to

★★ **4** Complete the text with *a*, *an* or *some* and these words.

apple	banana	~~bread~~
cheese	juice	tomatoes

Sam and Ella are having a picnic today.

They have ¹ 🥖 *some bread* and

² 🧀 .... .They have

³ 🍅 .... , too. Sam has

⁴ 🍌 .... , and Ella has

⁵ 🍎 .... .They also have

⁶ 🧃 ....

• Many/Much/A lot of

★ **5** Complete the questions with *How many/much*.

1 *How much* bread is there?
2 .... cheese is there?
3 .... apples are there?
4 .... sandwiches are there?
5 .... water is there?
6 .... bananas are there?

★★ **6** Look at the pictures. Answer the questions in Exercise 5 with *Not much/many* or *A lot of*.

1 *A lot of bread*   2 ....   3 ....

4 ....   5 ....   6 ....

★★ **7** Look at the pictures and write what they have. Use *much/many* or *A lot of*.

1 books
She has a lot of books.

2 money
....
....

3 apples
....
....

4 DVDs
....
....

Grammar Reference pages 120–121

Vocabulary • Adjectives

★ **(1)** **Read the sentences and mark the correct pictures.**

1 Fido is a very quiet dog.
2 Our car is always clean. It's never dirty.
3 This cup of tea is cold.
4 This is a very large beach ball.
5 This is a horrible beach.
6 This apple is disgusting.

1 a ☑ b ☐   2 a ☐ b ☐

3 a ☐ b ☐   4 a ☐ b ☐

5 a ☐ b ☐   6 a ☐ b ☐

★ **(2)** **Find 12 adjectives. Then label the pictures in Exercise 1.**

N	O	I	S	Y	D	X	G	D	Q
K	H	O	R	R	I	B	L	E	D
W	O	N	D	E	R	F	U	L	W
B	T	G	R	G	T	A	I	I	L
N	R	D	S	E	Y	W	E	C	A
T	S	I	M	A	L	Q	Y	I	R
C	L	E	A	N	H	U	A	O	G
O	E	I	L	H	T	I	N	U	E
L	N	E	L	C	N	E	R	S	A
D	I	S	G	U	S	T	I	N	G

Picture 1   a *quiet*   b ....
Picture 2   a .... b ....
Picture 3   a .... b ....
Picture 4   a .... b ....
Picture 5   a .... b ....
Picture 6   a .... b ....

★★ **(3)** **Put the letters in the correct order.**

1 It's a *hot* (oth) and sunny day.
2 I'm on the beach eating ....
   (uieidslco) ice cream.
3 We're staying in a .... (geral) hotel
   next to the beach.
4 There are a lot of .... (ysino) children
   playing with a beach ball.
5 The pool is .... (encal), and I go
   swimming every day.

★★ **(4)** **Write opposite sentences with these adjectives.**

cold	dirty	disgusting
horrible	quiet	~~small~~

1 My school is very large.
   My school is very small.
2 Our classroom's hot.

   ....

3 The food at school is delicious.

   ....

4 We're very noisy at lunchtime.

   ....

5 Dorothy is a wonderful singer.

   ....

6 The windows in our classroom are clean.

   ....

★★ **(5)** **Write true sentences. Use these words and/or your own ideas.**

guitars	horse	mouse
tea	trumpets	water

1 noisy / quiet instruments
   Trumpets are noisy instruments. Guitars are
   quiet instruments.
2 delicious / disgusting food

   ....

3 a hot / cold drink

   ....

4 a wonderful / horrible TV show

   ....

5 a small / large animal

   ....

6 a clean / dirty job

   ....

Workbook page 129

Speaking and Listening

★ **1** **Read the sentences. Write Waiter (W) or Customer (C).**

1 Are you ready to order?   W
2 I'd like a shrimp sandwich, please.   ....
3 I'll have a tomato salad, please.   ....
4 Would you like anything to drink?   ....
5 Can I have ice cream, please?   ....

★ **2** **Listen and read the conversation.**
22 **Match the people to the food.**

1 Frank
2 Beth's mom
3 Beth

 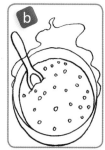 

Beth	I'm hungry.
Beth's mom	Me too! It's lunchtime. Let's go into this café.
Beth	Can we sit at the table next to the window? It's nicer than this one.
Beth's mom	I agree. It's quieter, too!
Waiter	Are you ready to order?
Beth's mom	Yes, we are. Frank, what would you like?
Frank	I'd like a ham and cheese sandwich, please.
Waiter	Would you like anything to drink?
Frank	A glass of orange juice, please.
Beth's mom	Beth?
Beth	A tuna salad for me, please. And orange juice too, please.
Waiter	Would you like some bread with that?
Beth	No, I'm OK, thanks.
Beth's mom	I'll have the soup, please. And can I have some water, please?
Waiter	Yes, of course.

★★ **3** **Read the conversation again. Are the statements true (T) or false (F)?**

1 Frank, Beth and her mom go to
 a restaurant.   F
2 They sit next to the window.   ....
3 They order food for lunch.   ....
4 Frank and Beth ask for smoothies.   ....
5 Beth would like some bread.   ....
6 Beth's mom would like some water.   ....

★★ **4** **Complete the conversation. Then listen and check.**
23

drink	have	ice cream	I'd	OK	~~order~~

Waiter	Are you ready to ¹ *order*?
Customer	Yes. ² .... like a tuna salad, please.
Waiter	Would you like some bread?
Customer	No, I'm ³ .... , thanks.
Waiter	Would you like anything to ⁴ ....?
Customer	I'll ⁵ .... orange juice, please.
Waiter	Would you like anything else?
Customer	I'd like some ⁶ .... , please.
Waiter	Yes, of course.
Customer	Thank you.

★★★ **5** **Look at the menu. Write a conversation between a waiter and a customer. Use the model in Exercise 4.**

● *Main course*

tuna salad   *pasta with chicken*
burger and fries   *ham and cheese pizza*

● *Drinks*

water   *orange juice*   *smoothie*

● *Desserts*

chocolate cake   ice cream   fruit salad

Speaking and Listening page 134

Grammar • Comparatives

★ (1) Write the comparative form of these adjectives in the correct column.

clean	delicious	~~dirty~~	disgusting
easy	funny	hot	~~interesting~~
large	~~nice~~	~~small~~	white

Short adjectives	Short adjectives ending in -e
[1] *smaller*, [2] .... , [3]	[4] *nicer*, [5] .... , [6] ....
Adjectives ending in -y	**Long adjectives**
[7] *dirtier*, [8] .... , [9]	[10] *more interesting*, [11] .... , [12] ....

★ (2) Complete the sentences with the comparative form of the adjectives.

1 The Station Hotel is *smaller* (small) than the Park Hotel.
2 This café is .... (noisy) than the restaurant.
3 The French menu is .... (difficult) to understand than the English menu.
4 The waiter is .... (young) than the customer.
5 Lunch is .... (cheap) than dinner.
6 These salads are .... (good) than the pizzas.

★ (3) Rewrite the sentences in Exercise 2 with these adjectives.

| bad | easy | expensive | ~~large~~ | old | quiet |

1 The Park Hotel *is larger than* the Station Hotel.
2 The restaurant .... the café.
3 The English menu .... the French menu.
4 The customer .... the waiter.
5 Dinner .... lunch.
6 The pizzas .... these salads.

★★ (4) Complete the text with the comparative form of the adjectives.

My family isn't big. There's just my mom, my sister and me. I'm 13, and she's 11. My sister's [1] *younger* (young) than me, but she's [2] .... (tall). We live in a small apartment. I have a [3] .... (big) bedroom than she does, but her room is [4] .... (clean) and [5] .... (neat). At school, we like different subjects. I'm [6] .... (good) at English and French, but she finds languages [7] .... (difficult) than I do. She likes PE, and she's a fast runner. She's [8] .... (fast) than me. She has a lot of friends, and she's [9] .... (popular) than me! She's [10] .... (noisy), too!

★★ (5) Compare these things. Use the adjectives.

1 red car (expensive)   2 green bag (small)
  blue car (cheap)   yellow bag (large)

3 Sam's bike (new)   4 June's phone (noisy)
  Tom's bike (old)   Ella's phone (quiet)

5 Sam's T-shirt (dirty)
  Dan's T-shirt (clean)

1 *The blue car is cheaper than the red car.*
  The red car is more expensive than the blue car.
2 ....
....
3 ....
....
4 ....
....
5 ....
....

Grammar Reference pages 120–121

Reading

1 Read the profile. Choose the correct sentence.

1 Jamie Oliver is a farmer.
2 Jamie Oliver is a TV chef.
3 Jamie Oliver is a school teacher.

> **Brain Trainer**
>
> **When you see a new word similar to a word you know, guess the meaning. Find *cooking* in the text. What do you think it means?**
>
> Verb   Noun
> *cook*   *a cook*
>
> **Now read the profile.**

Jamie Oliver is a busy man. What does he do? He's a chef, and he loves cooking. He has his own TV shows. He writes cookbooks. He has a website with a blog and a lot of ideas for things to cook. He gives cooking lessons. He has many restaurants.

Jamie wants everyone to eat and enjoy good food. Cooking is fun, and good food helps you live a long and happy life. He also works to help children and young people. His TV shows prove that food can be delicious *and* good for you.

Jamie cooks dishes from different countries on his TV shows. His *Jamie's Italian* restaurants serve food from Italy. His *Fifteen* restaurants are special. Some young people leave school and can't find work. Every year, fifteen of these young people start work in Jamie's restaurants and learn to cook. Some of them are now chefs and have their own restaurants.

2 Read the profile again. Are the statements true (T) or false (F)?

1 Jamie doesn't do very much.   *F*
2 He writes books about geography.   ....
3 He has a lot of restaurants.   ....
4 He wants people to eat well.   ....
5 He helps some young people without jobs. ....

3 Read the profile again. Answer the questions.

1 What is on Jamie's website?
A blog and a lot of ideas for things to cook.
2 How does good food help you?
....
3 Which restaurants cook food from Italy?
....
4 How many young people start work at *Fifteen* every year?
....
5 Do some of these young people have their own restaurants now?
....

Listening

1 Listen and check the correct answer.
24
What is *Young Masterchef*?
1 A TV cooking competition for children. ☐
2 A restaurant in New York. ☐
3 A special school for chefs. ☐

2 Listen again. Choose the correct answers.
24
1 George is …
a this year's winner.   b last year's winner.
2 He's …
a 11 years old.   b 12 years old.
3 George is cooking …
a carrot soup.   b tomato soup.
4 His favorite dish is …
a strawberry ice cream.
b strawberry cheesecake.
5 George wants to have his own …
a restaurant.   b TV show.

3 Listen again. Answer the questions.
24
1 How old are the children on *Young Masterchef*?
....
2 Who do the children cook for?
....
3 Is George cooking today?
....
4 What is George cooking with the fish?
....
5 What does George want to be?
....

Writing • Instructions

1 **Number the sentences in order. Then rewrite them using *First, Then* and *Finally*.**

toothpaste — toothbrush

1 ☐ Brush your teeth for two minutes.
☐ Rinse your brush and put it back in the cup.
☐1 Put toothpaste and some water on your toothbrush.

1 *First, put toothpaste and some water on your toothbrush.*

2 ....
....

3 ....
....

dog bowl — Dog — can

2 ☐ Give the bowl to the dog.
☐ Open a can of dog food.
☐ Put some food in the dog bowl.

....
....
....
....

2 **Complete the instructions with these verbs.**

| add | blend | ~~chop~~ | enjoy | pour |

1 *Chop* the banana.
2 .... some raspberries and yogurt.
3 .... the ingredients for a minute.
4 .... the mixture into a glass.
5 .... your smoothie with some friends.

3 **Read the recipe and mark the correct picture.**

a ☐   b ☐   c ☐

4 **Read the recipe again. Answer the questions.**

1 How many slices of bread are there?
....

2 Is there any mayonnaise on the bread?
....

3 What meat is in this sandwich?
....

4 What do you add first, the tomato or the chicken?
....

5 What do people often eat with the sandwich?
....

5 **Now write a recipe for your favorite sandwich. Use *First, Then, Finally*. Use the recipe guide below, and the recipe in Exercise 3 to help you.**

Make a .... sandwich
Ingredients
bread, …
First, ...
....
....
....
....
....
....

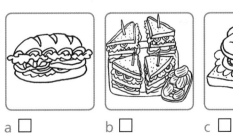

Make a club sandwich

Ingredients

• three slices of white bread
• mayonnaise
• chicken
• tomato
• lettuce

First, toast the three slices of bread.
Then put mayonnaise on each slice.
Add the chicken to one slice of bread. Put another slice of bread on top of the chicken.
Put the tomato and lettuce on the second slice of bread. Put the last slice of bread on top.
Finally, cut the club sandwich into four pieces. Put it on a plate and enjoy it with some chips.

Check ②

Grammar

1 Write the rules. Use *You must* or *You mustn't*.

> • tell someone where you are going ✓
> • walk on your own ✗
> • take food and water ✓
> • go in foggy weather ✗
> • take a map ✓

Rules for hiking in the mountains

0 *You must tell someone where you are going.*
1 ....
2 ....
3 ....
4 ....

.... / 4 points

2 Complete the sentences with the Present simple or Present continuous.

0 We often *go* (go) to the zoo in the summer.
1 .... you .... (wear) your hat now?
2 Why .... they always ....
(get up) early?
3 When .... he usually ....
(finish) school?
4 .... she .... (do) gymnastics now?
5 We .... (not play) tennis on Sundays.
6 I................(watch) a news show at the moment.

.... / 6 points

3 Choose the correct options. Then complete the text with *much* or *many*.

How much food do we have? There ⁰(*isn't*)/
aren't much pasta, and there ¹ *isn't* / *aren't*
.... shrimp. There ² *isn't* / *aren't*
.... broccoli, and there ³ *isn't* / *aren't*
.... carrots. There ⁴ *is* / *are* a lot of eggs,
but there ⁵ *isn't* / *aren't* .... ice cream.

.... / 5 points

4 Look at the pictures. Complete the sentences with these phrases. Then put the word in parentheses in the correct place.

go ice skating	~~go kayaking~~
go mountain biking	go rollerblading
go climbing	play the guitar

0 (often) He *often goes kayaking* when it's sunny.
1 (never) She ....
when it's foggy.
2 (always) They ....
when it's cloudy.
3 (usually) He ....
when it's raining.
4 (hardly ever) He ....
when it's windy.
5 (sometimes) They ....
when it's cold.

.... / 5 points

Vocabulary

5 Look at the pictures and complete the sentences.

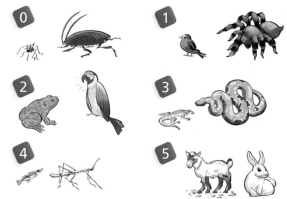

0 The *spider* is smaller than the *hissing cockroach*.
1 The .... is larger than
the ....
2 The .... is noisier than
the ....
3 The .... is longer than
the ....
4 The .... is smaller than
the ....
5 The .... is dirtier than
the ....

/ 5 points

6 **Label the pizzas.**

0 b*anana* pizza
1 c .... and h .... pizza
2 t .... and s .... pizza
3 c .... and t .... pizza
4 s .... and b .... pizza
5 s .... and e .... pizza

/ 5 points

Speaking

7 **Match the sentences (1–5) to the responses (a–e).**

0 I have the best grades in the class!   0
1 Do you like kayaking?
2 The football game isn't on TV today.
3 I have tickets for *X Factor* next week.
4 I can hear an insect. Can you see it?
5 I like dancing.

0 Wow! That's wonderful! Good job!
a How amazing! Lucky you!
b Me too! I love it.
c No. I don't like water sports.
d Yes. It's just a mosquito.
e Really? Oh! Why not?

/ 5 points

8 **Choose the correct options to complete the conversation.**

Waiter   Are you ready to order?
Mom   Yes, we are.
Waiter   What ⁰ *would you like* / *do you want*?
Sarah   ¹ *Give me* / *I'll have* the spaghetti, please.
Mom   And ² *I'd like* / *I want* the burger
         with fries, please.
Waiter   ³ *What do you want* / *Would you like*
         anything to drink?
Sarah   ⁴ *Can I have* / *Give me* a glass of
         orange juice, please?
Mom   And ⁵ *I drink* / *I'd like* water, please.
Waiter   Yes, of course. Is that all?
Mom   Yes, thank you.

/ 5 points

Translation

9 **Translate the sentences.**

1 She hardly ever goes hiking in winter.

....
....

2 Are they feeding the rabbits?

....
....

3 How much bread do we have in the fridge?

....
....

4 Autumn is usually foggier than spring.

....
....

5 You must be quiet in the library.

....
....

/ 5 points

Dictation

10 **Listen and write.**
25

/ 5 points

7 Modern History

Vocabulary • Ordinal numbers, years, dates

★ **1** Find the ordinal numbers in the word snake. Then write them in the correct sentence.

seventhfourthfirstsixththirdsecondfifth

Dates the Harry Potter books go on sale:

1 1997   The *first* Harry Potter book.
2 1998   The .... book.
3 1999   The .... book.
4 2000   The .... book.
5 2003   The .... book.
6 2005   The .... book.
7 2007   The .... book.

★ **2** Choose the correct options.

1 May thirty-first
   May 13 / May 31
2 June ninth
   June 9 / June 19
3 July seventeenth
   July 17 / July 7
4 November twenty-second
   November 2 / November 22
5 March third, nineteen thirty-two
   March 3, 1932 / March 3, 1952
6 October fifteenth, two thousand ten
   October 13, 2001 / October 15, 2010

★★ **3** Complete the dates.

1 January first, two thousand
   January 1, *2000*
2 April second, nineteen sixty-six
   April ...., ...
3 February twenty-ninth, two thousand twelve
   February ...., ...
4 December tenth, nineteen eleven
   December ...., ...
5 September fourth, nineteen forty-four
   September ...., ...

★★ **4** Write the dates.

1 March third, nineteen thirty-two *3/3/1932*
2 September twenty-seventh, two thousand eleven ....
3 February fourth, nineteen sixteen
   ....
4 October eighteenth, nineteen eighty-four
   ....
5 April twentieth, two thousand one
   ....
6 January thirteenth, nineteen fifty-seven
   ....

★★ **5** Complete the sentences with the correct dates.

11/11/1918   8/4/2012   7/20/1969

5/6/1994   12/14/1911   3/9/1959

1 On *November eleventh, nineteen eighteen*, World War I ends.
2 On..,
   Michael Phelps wins his eighteenth gold Olympic medal for swimming.
3 On ....,
   the first man walks on the moon.
4 On ....,
   the channel tunnel opens between France and England.
5 On ....,
   Roald Amundsen reaches the South Pole.
6 On ....,
   the Barbie doll goes on sale.

Workbook page 130

Reading

1 Read the text quickly. Mark the correct description. ★

1 ☐ This is from Alice's letter.
2 ☐ This is from Alice's schoolbook.
3 ☐ This is from Alice's diary.

Brain Trainer

Look at the pictures. They often help you understand a text.

Now do Exercise 2.

---

2 Read the text again. Number the pictures in order. ★

a ☐

b ☐
underground tunnel

c ☐

d ☐

e ☐

3 Read the text again. Match the sentence beginnings (1–6) to the endings (a–f). ★★

1 Tom likes
2 Alice is Tom's
3 Alice's diaries are
4 In 1940, Alice was
5 Alice's mom was
6 Alice's dad was

a grandmother.
b a good cook.
c 12 years old.
d family history.
e in France.
f from World War II.

4 Answer the questions. ★★

1 How many wartime diaries does Tom have?
He has seven diaries.
2 What is the date of the diary entry?
....
3 How many planes were over London on September 7?
....
4 Why were hundreds of people in the underground tunnel?
....
5 Why wasn't lunch nice?
....
6 Why is Alice's mom happy?
....

Alice

> *I like family history. We have the wartime diaries of my grandmother, Alice. There are seven diaries from 1939 to 1945, one for each year of World War II. This is an extract from her diary when she was twelve.*

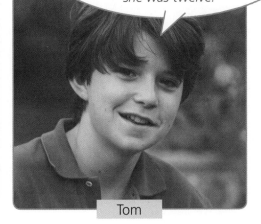
Tom

London, September 8, 1940

Last night was scary. We were in the underground tunnel all night. They stop the trains when the planes come over so people can hide there. There were fifteen planes last night. There were hundreds of people with us. It was noisy, but we were safe. I was worried about our house, but it was still there in the morning!

Lunch wasn't very nice today. There wasn't any meat, and the vegetables were old. Mom's a good cook, but we can't buy much food. I can't remember the last time there were bananas in our house.

There's some good news. There was a letter from Daddy this afternoon. He was in France, but he's back in England now. He's fine, and he's coming home. Mom's very happy.

Grammar • Past simple: *to be*

★ **1** **Complete the sentences with *was/were*.**

1 They *were* in the supermarket an hour ago.
2 I .... at my grandparents' house last weekend.
3 Carol and Terry .... at the train station yesterday morning.
4 The juice .... in the fridge.
5 She .... in her room a minute ago.
6 We .... in Hawaii last summer.

★ **2** **Rewrite the sentences and questions for yesterday.**

Today	Yesterday
1 Are your friends at school?	*Were your friends at school?*
2 My mom isn't at work.	....
3 Is your dad at home?	....
4 We aren't in the classroom.	....
5 Is your favorite show on TV?	....
6 I'm at the swimming pool.	....
7 There isn't much food in the fridge.	....
8 Are there any children in the park?	....

★★ **3** **Look at the pictures. Complete the text with *was, were, wasn't* or *weren't*.**

Lizzie's blog:
I ¹ *was* busy on Saturday. In the morning my mom and I ² .... shopping downtown. We ³ .... there long because the weather ⁴ .... terrible. In the afternoon I ⁵ .... with my friends at the movies. We ⁶ .... happy because the movie ⁷ .... silly and boring. It ⁸ .... good. On Sunday I ⁹ .... at home with my family. We ¹⁰ .... in the backyard because it ¹¹ .... sunny.

• There was/There were

★ **4** **Choose the correct options.**

1 There (wasn't) / weren't any music at the party.
2 There *was* / *were* a lot of cars outside the school last Saturday.
3 There *was* / *were* an interesting history class yesterday.
4 There *wasn't* / *weren't* any Internet or TV twenty years ago.

★★ **5** **Complete the questions with *Was/Were there … ?* Then write true answers.**

1 *Was there* any English homework last week? *Yes, there was. / No, there wasn't.*
2 .... any snow last winter?
....
3 .... any good shows on TV last night?
....
4 .... many students in your class last year?
....
5 .... any rain yesterday?
....

★★ **6** **Look at the pictures. Correct the sentences.**

1 There were some girls at the beach last summer.
There weren't any girls at the beach.
There were some boys.
2 There were some boys at the café yesterday.
....
3 There was a post office here two years ago.
....
4 There was a cat in the backyard ten minutes ago.
....

Grammar Reference pages 122–123

Vocabulary • Regular verbs

★ **1** Match the verbs (1–6) to the pictures (a–f).

1 call c   3 talk   5 work
2 answer   4 study   6 like

★ **2** Find the verbs.

ask	close	invent	listen	stop	travel

C	L	O	S	E	F	G
K	A	L	T	M	N	D
A	S	L	O	I	Z	O
B	K	A	P	N	I	U
X	T	R	A	V	E	L
L	I	S	T	E	N	P
W	R	T	C	N	L	S
G	R	E	W	T	O	E

★ **3** Choose the correct pronunciation.
26 Then listen and check.

1 traveled	/d/	/ɪd/	/t/
2 stopped	/d/	/ɪd/	/t/
3 invented	/d/	/ɪd/	/t/
4 asked	/d/	/ɪd/	/t/
5 listened	/d/	/ɪd/	/t/
6 closed	/d/	/ɪd/	/t/

★★ **4** Complete the sentences with the words from Exercise 3.

1 John Logie Baird *invented* television.
2 I .... to the story on the radio yesterday. ·
3 They .... to Russia last year.
4 The stores .... at 8 p.m.
5 We .... a lot of questions.
6 The train .... at Edison Park station.

★★ **5** Match the verbs (1–6) to the phrases (a–f).

1 ask   a a window
2 listen   b to music
3 close   c to the US
4 call   d a question
5 travel   e in a school
6 work   f a friend

★★ **6** Complete the conversation with these words.

answer	asked	called	close	like
listen	stop	studying	talk	~~working~~

Elsa Where's mom?
Dad She's ¹ *working* at the hospital. Why?
Elsa A man ² .... and wanted to ³ .... to her.
Dad Who was it?
Elsa I don't know. I ⁴ .... him, but he didn't ⁵ ....
Colin Can you ⁶ .... the door, please? I'm doing my homework and I don't want to ⁷ .... to your conversation.
Elsa What are you ⁸ .... ?
Colin English.
Elsa Do you ⁹ .... English?
Colin Yes, I do. It's my favorite subject.
Dad Elsa, ¹⁰ .... talking to Colin and let him do his homework.
Elsa OK, Dad.

Workbook page 130

Chatroom Talking about the past

Speaking and Listening

> **Brain Trainer**
>
> Practice and learn the set phrases and expressions that make talking easier.
> Read the conversation in Exercise 1 and find the phrases in the list.
>
> | | | |
> |---|---|---|
> | Cool! | Great. | Hang on. |
> | Here we are! | Hi, guys! | I know. |
> | Let's go! | Me too! | See you later! |
> | Yuck! | Yum! | Yes, of course. |
> | What a pain! | | |
>
> **Now do Exercise 1.**

★ **1** Listen and read the conversation. <u>Underline</u>
27   the past-time words and phrases.

Beth   Hi, Frank!
Frank Hi! Where were you <u>last night</u>? I called, but you didn't answer!
Beth   I was at the gym yesterday, and my phone wasn't on. Sorry. What are you doing here?
Frank There's a special showing of *ET* at the movie theater this afternoon. It was popular in the 1980s. I love it.
Beth   Me too!
Frank I want to see it. Do you want to come, too?
Beth   Yes, of course. I'd love to.
Frank Oh no!
Beth   What is it?
Frank I got the time wrong. The movie started half an hour ago.
Beth   And you got the day wrong. It was showing last week!
Frank What a pain! Let's watch a DVD at home instead.

★ **2** Read the conversation again. Correct the <u>underlined</u> time phrases.

1 Frank phoned Beth <u>this morning</u>.
  Frank phoned Beth last night.
2 *ET* was popular <u>in the 1960s</u>.
  ....
3 The movie started <u>two minutes ago</u>.
  ....
4 The movie was showing <u>yesterday</u>.
  ....

★★ **3** Complete the sentences.

afternoon	~~May~~	for an hour	two weeks

1 We moved last *May*.
2 I visited the doctor .... ago.
3 I waited at the station ....
4 They played basketball this ....

★★ **4** Match the questions (1–6) to the answers (a–f).
28   Then listen and check.

1 When was your last vacation?   c
2 Where were you last summer?
3 How long was the flight to Orlando?
4 How long was the vacation?
5 Who were you with?
6 What was your favorite day?

a I was there with my whole family.
b We were on the plane for two hours.
c It was in July, about eight months ago.
d I loved the day we were at Disney World.
e We were there for two weeks.
f We were in Orlando, Florida.

★★ **5** Write a conversation about your friend Amy's vacation. Use the information below.

Amy's summer vacation

When?	last August
Where?	to Costa Rica
How long the trip?	8 hours by plane
Who with?	my family
How long the vacation?	10 days
Favorite day?	the last day—we went snorkeling

Speaking and Listening page 135

Grammar • Past simple regular: affirmative and negative

★ 1 Read the sentences and write *Past simple* or *Present simple*.

1 I asked the teacher a question. *Past simple*
2 She doesn't watch TV in the morning.
....
3 We like going to the movies. ....
4 They didn't bike to school. ....
5 He studied Spanish and French. ....
6 You didn't call me. ....

★ 2 Complete the table.

Infinitive	Past simple affirmative	Past simple negative
1 answer	*answered*	*didn't answer*
2 travel	....	....
3 dance	....	....
4 jump	....	....
5 start	....	....
6 study	....	....

★ 3 Complete the sentences with the Past simple of the verbs.

1 They *watched* (watch) an awesome movie.
2 You .... (not listen) to the teacher.
3 We .... (travel) for six hours.
4 He .... (not cook) dinner.
5 I .... (play) baseball with some friends.
6 She .... (visit) her grandmother.

★ 4 Look at the pictures. Complete the sentences with these phrases. Use the correct form of the Past simple.

listen to jazz music	~~paint some fruit~~
play soccer	start a weather project
study plants	study the presidents

1 *In art, she painted some fruit.*
2 ....
3 ....
4 ....
5 ....
6 ....

Grammar Reference pages 122–123

★★ 5 Look at the pictures. Write sentences about Donna when she was young. Use the Past simple form of these verbs.

climb	listen	~~play~~	study
clean up	travel	watch	

1 *She didn't play tennis.*
2 ....
3 ....
4 ....
5 ....
6 ....
7 ....

art

PE

science

history

geography

music

Reading

1 Match the photos (1–3) to the headlines (a–c).

 Robber Escapes by Parachute

 On Top of the World

 THE FAIRY TALE WEDDING

2 Read the articles. Match the photos (1–3) and headlines (a–c) to the articles.

1 ..... . Photo ☐

On May 26, 1953, two of the British expedition climbed all day, but they didn't reach the top of the mountain. The next two days were cold and windy. On May 28, a group of men started the climb. [1] .... At 11:30 the next morning, New Zealander Edmund Hillary, and Tenzing Norgay from Nepal, reached the top of Mount Everest. [2] ....

2 ..... . Photo ☐

On November 24, 1971, a man boarded a plane from Portland to Seattle. [3] .... The man handed a note to the flight attendant. The note said, "I have a bomb in my bag. Give me $200,000 and some parachutes, and nobody gets hurt." The plane landed in Seattle, and the man received the money and the parachutes. Then he ordered the pilot to fly to Mexico, and later he jumped off the plane using his parachute. [4] ....

3 ..... . Photo ☐

On Friday, April 29, 2011, Prince William married Kate Middleton. He is the grandson of the queen of England. [5] .... It was a beautiful wedding. [6] .... Thousands of people traveled to London and waited in the streets to see them. Millions of people around the world watched the wedding on TV.

3 Read the articles again. Six sentences are missing. Write the sentence letter in the correct place.

a He was around 40 years old, and he looked like any other passenger.
b They studied together at St. Andrews University in Scotland.
c They camped on the mountain that night.
d There were hundreds of people in Westminster Abbey.
e They stayed only 15 minutes at the top.
f This was one of the most mysterious robberies in US history.

4 Answer the questions.

1 Were Hillary and Norgay British?
No, they weren't.
2 What date were Hillary and Norgay at the top of Mount Everest?
....
3 What did the man on the plane look like?
....
4 What did the man do with the parachute?
....
5 Where was the wedding?
....
6 How many people were in the streets?
....

Listening

1 Listen and circle the correct date.
29
1 January 1, 2000
2 September 11, 2001
3 November 4, 2008

2 Listen and answer the questions.
29
1 Where was Katy?
She was at home in Kansas City.
2 Who was Katy with?
....
3 How old was Katy?
....
4 Where was Toby?
....
5 Who was Toby with?
....
6 Where were the fireworks?
....

Writing • An essay

1 **Rewrite the sentences with the correct punctuation: commas, periods, question marks or exclamation points.**

1 Where does your family come from
  Where does your family come from?
2 I was born on January 14 1999
  ....
3 My grandparents came from Lamia a small town in Greece
  ....
4 Were your parents in school together
  ....
5 My grandparents aunts uncles and cousins all lived in that house
  ....
  ....

2 **Read the essay. Match the sentence beginnings (1–5) to the endings (a–e).**

1 Bonnie   a come from Dallas.
2 Her mom   b live in Dublin.
3 Her dad   c was born in Tampa.
4 Her grandparents d didn't stay in Dallas.
5 Her aunt and uncle e left his country many years ago.

My family history

My name's Bonnie, and I was born in Tampa, a city in Florida. I still live in Tampa with my family, but my parents weren't born here.

My mom grew up in Dallas, Texas, but she moved when she got a job in Tampa. She met my dad at a party. My mother's parents were from Dallas, too. I think her family lived in Dallas for many years.

My dad's family is Irish. My dad left Ireland when he was 21 because there wasn't any work there. My aunt and uncle live in Dublin, but I don't know much about my Irish family.

3 **Read the essay again. Correct the sentences.**

1 Tampa is a city in Texas.
  Tampa is a city in Florida.
2 Bonnie's parents were born in Tampa.
  ....
3 Her mom moved to Ireland.
  ....
4 Her parents met at work.
  ....
5 Her mom's family comes from the country.
  ....
6 Her dad's family is Portuguese.
  ....

4 **Answer the questions and take notes about your family.**

Paragraph 1   Me
• Where were you born?
• Where do you live now?

Paragraph 2   My mom and her family
• Where is your mom from?
• Was her family from this place?

Paragraph 3   My dad and his family
• Where was your dad born?
• Was his family from this place?

5 **Now write an essay about your family history. Use the model in Exercise 2 and your notes from Exercise 4 to help you.**

  ....
  ....
  ....
  ....
  ....
  ....
  ....
  ....
  ....
  ....
  ....

8 Travel

Vocabulary • Means of transportation

★ **1** Label the pictures.

bike	bus	car	scooter	~~train~~	subway

1 *train* 2 .... 3 ....

4 .... 5 .... 6 ....

★ **2** Complete the crossword.

boat	bus	canoe	~~helicopter~~
truck	motorcycle	plane	

Across

3   4   5   7

Down

1 2 6

⁵ h e l i c o p ⁶ t e r

★★ **3** Complete the transportation groups.

Name two types of …

1 water transportation *boat* ....
2 motor transportation you can ride

....

3 air transportation

....

4 rail transportation that carries a lot of people

....

5 road transportation you can drive

....

★★ **4** Complete the sentences with these verbs.

~~drives~~	flies	ride	sails	takes

1 My mom *drives* her car to work every day.
2 I .... my bike to school in the morning.
3 Susie often .... the bus downtown.
4 In the summer my dad .... his boat around the Caribbean.
5 The police officer .... the helicopter in case of an accident.

★★ **5** Read the text. Choose the correct options.

In my family we all travel to school or work in different ways. My mom drives to work in her ¹ *car*. My dad has a ² .... because he transports fruits and vegetables to his store. My older sister rides her ³ .... to the airport. She flies small ⁴ .... to and from different places in the state. My brother is 16, and he rides a ⁵ .... to school. He wants a ⁶ .... when he is 17 because it's faster. My friends and I go to school on the school ⁷ .... There's a stop near my house.

1 a helicopter   b boat   c̄ car
2 a van   b subway   c train
3 a bike   b boat   c canoe
4 a trains   b planes   c subway
5 a truck   b canoe   c scooter
6 a bike   b motorcycle c truck
7 a bus   b van   c boat

Workbook page 131

Reading

★ **1** Read the websites. Match the photos (a–c) to the paragraphs (1–3).

★ **2** Read the websites again. Write *Mark*, *Charlie* or *Sarah*.

1 *Charlie* is American.
2 .... is Scottish.
3 .... is English.
4 .... started when he/she was 4 years old.
5 .... started when he/she was 10.
6 .... started when he/she was 12.

★★ **3** Read the websites again. Are the statements true (T) or false (F)?

1 Mark biked around the world when
  he was 15.   *F*
2 Mark's video diary was for TV.   ....
3 Charlie has flying lessons with his dad.   ....
4 Charlie started flying in 2008.   ....
5 Sarah was 17 in 2009.   ....
6 Sarah was the first girl to win the
  Ginetta Junior Championship.   ....

★★ **4** Answer the questions.

1 Where did Mark bike in 1998?
  He biked from John O'Groats to Land's End.
2 How long was Mark's trip around the world?
  ....
3 Where were Charlie's flying lessons?
  ....
4 At what age can Charlie fly solo?
  ....
5 At what age can you drive in the UK?
  ....
6 What does Sarah want to do?
  ....

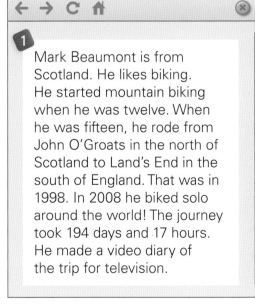

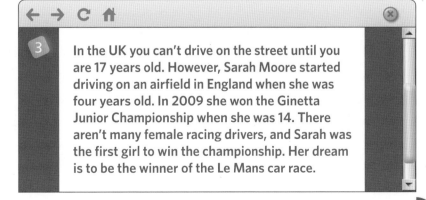

2 Charlie Goldfarb enjoys flying planes. In the summer of 2008, Charlie's father arranged some flying lessons for him near his home in California in the US, and he loved it. He was only ten years old. He is very good, but he can't fly solo until he is sixteen years old.

1 Mark Beaumont is from Scotland. He likes biking. He started mountain biking when he was twelve. When he was fifteen, he rode from John O'Groats in the north of Scotland to Land's End in the south of England. That was in 1998. In 2008 he biked solo around the world! The journey took 194 days and 17 hours. He made a video diary of the trip for television.

3 In the UK you can't drive on the street until you are 17 years old. However, Sarah Moore started driving on an airfield in England when she was four years old. In 2009 she won the Ginetta Junior Championship when she was 14. There aren't many female racing drivers, and Sarah was the first girl to win the championship. Her dream is to be the winner of the Le Mans car race.

Grammar • Past simple irregular: affirmative and negative

Brain Trainer

There are many irregular Past simple verbs. Do not try to learn them all at once. Learn three or four every day.

Now do Exercise 1.

★ **1** Write the verbs in the Past simple.

1 go   *went*
2 think   ....
3 take   ....
4 get   ....
5 buy   ....
6 understand ....
7 have   ....
8 do   ....

★ **2** Complete the sentences with the negative form of the Past simple.

1 You *didn't understand* (understand) the question.
2 She .... (go) shopping.
3 I .... (ride) my scooter.
4 They .... (eat) breakfast.
5 He .... (drive) the car.
6 We .... (do) our homework.

★★ **3** Complete the sentences with the correct form of the verbs.

1 I *buy* flowers every week. Last week I *bought* some roses. (buy)
2 He usually .... the bus to work, but last week he .... the train. (take)
3 Last summer we .... to Spain by boat. We .... there every year. (go)
4 They always .... chicken for lunch on Sundays, but they .... fish today. (have)
5 She .... Tony on his bike this morning, but she usually .... him in the evenings. (see)
6 I usually .... milk for breakfast, but when we were on vacation, I .... orange juice. (drink)

Grammar Reference pages 124–125

★★ **4** Rewrite the sentences. Use the Past simple negative.

1 I did all my homework this week.
   I didn't do all my homework this week.
2 They bought an old white van.
   ....
3 My dad gave me five dollars.
   ....
4 I thought about our visit to Philadelphia.
   ....
5 She ate pizza for lunch.
   ....

★★ **5** Write Past simple sentences.

1 we / go / to the movies yesterday
   We went to the movies yesterday.
2 I / meet / my friend at the bus stop
   ....
3 my friend / give / me her old magazine
   ....
4 Mom / buy / a new camera
   ....
5 Dad / get / a new bike last week
   ....
6 they / have / lunch in a café
   ....

★★★ **6** Complete the text with the Past simple form of the verbs.

Last weekend we visited an old mansion. My dad ¹ *drove* (drive), and the trip ² .... (take) an hour and a half. We ³ .... (not get) there until ten thirty. We ⁴ .... (spend) the morning in the gardens. My brother ⁵ .... (see) a beautiful yellow bird, but I ⁶ .... (not see) it. There ⁷ .... (be) a café, but we ⁸ .... (not have) lunch there. We ⁹ .... (have) a picnic in the gardens. In the afternoon, we ¹⁰ .... (go) into the mansion. There ¹¹ .... (be) a lot of rooms to see. I ¹² .... (not like) the bathrooms, but I ¹³ .... (think) the kitchens were interesting. At the end of the day, I ¹⁴ .... (buy) a small key ring from the souvenir shop. We ¹⁵ .... (have) a wonderful day.

Vocabulary • Clothes

★ **1** **Label the clothes.**

| hat | pajamas | pants | scarf |
| shoes | skirt | ~~sneakers~~ | |

1 *sneakers*   2 ....   3 ....

4 ....   5 ....

6 ....   7 ....

★ **2** **Match the descriptions (1–4) to the people (a–d).**

Robin   Carly   Alexa   Sam

1 We're in the mountains in Vermont. It's cold, and I'm wearing a coat and boots.   *c Carly*
2 I'm camping with my family near the beach. I'm wearing shorts and a T-shirt.   ....
3 It's autumn, and it isn't very warm. I'm wearing jeans and a sweater.   ....
4 I'm on vacation in Miami. It's hot, and I'm wearing a dress and sandals.   ....

★★ **3** **Look at the pictures in Exercise 2. Complete the descriptions.**

| boots | coat | ~~dress~~ | jeans |
| sandals | shorts | sweater | T-shirt |

1 Alexa is wearing a *dress* and ....
2 Robin is wearing ....
   and a ....
3 Carly is wearing a ....
   and ....
4 Sam is wearing ....
   and a ....

★★ **4** **Write the correct words. Then add your own ideas.**

| coat | jeans | pajamas | shoes | ~~shorts~~ | skirt |

1 You wear these in summer.
   shorts   ....
2 You put this on to go outside in winter.
   ....
3 You wear these on your feet.
   ....
4 Boys don't wear this.
   ....
5 You wear these on your legs.
   ....
6 Something you wear in bed.
   ....

★★★ **5** **Write true answers.**

1 What are you wearing today?
   ....
2 What do you usually wear to school?
   ....
3 What do you wear at the beach?
   ....
4 What do you wear at night?
   ....
5 What do you wear on your feet?
   ....
6 What clothes do you have for parties?
   ....
7 What are your favorite clothes?
   ....

Workbook page 131

Chatroom Talking on the phone

Speaking and Listening

★ **1** Match the sentence beginnings (1–6) to the
30 endings (a–f) to make phrases for talking on
the phone. Then listen and check.

1	This	a	on.
2	Is	b	here he is.
3	Who's	c	is Beth.
4	Hold	d	this Frank?
5	Can I speak	e	this?
6	Just a minute …	f	to Frank, please?

★ **2** Listen and read the conversation. <u>Underline</u>
31 phrases from Exercise 1. Which phrases in
Exercise 1 are not in the conversation?

Frank's dad	Hello.
Beth	Hi. This is Beth. Is this Frank?
Frank's dad	Hello, Beth. No, it's Frank's dad.
Beth	Hello. Can I speak to Frank, please?
Frank's dad	Yes, of course. Frank! Just a minute … here he is.
Frank	Hi, Beth.
Beth	Hi, Frank. Listen, I had a piano lesson today, so I missed geography. Do we have any homework?
Frank	No, we don't, but Miss Woods gave us our books back. I have your homework book. I can bring it over to your house now.
Beth	That would be great! Thanks.
Frank	See you in a minute. Bye.
Beth	Bye.

★★ **3** Read the conversation again. Answer
the questions.

1 Who makes the phone call?
Beth makes the phone call.
2 Who answers the phone?
....
3 Who does Beth want to speak to?
....
4 Why wasn't Beth in geography class?
....
5 Why does Frank have Beth's homework book?
....
6 Where does Frank go at the end of
the conversation?
....

★★ **4** Complete the conversation with these words.
32 Then listen and check.

fine	~~Owen~~	Sally	swimming pool	two o'clock

Girl	Hello. Can I speak to ¹ *Owen*, please?
Boy	Hi, this is Owen. Is this Lettie?
Girl	No, it's ² ....
Boy	Oh. Hi, Sally. How are you?
Girl	I'm ³ .... , thanks. I'm going to the ⁴ .... this afternoon. Do you want to come, too?
Boy	Yes, I'd love to. What time are you going?
Girl	Let's meet there at ⁵ ....
Boy	Great! See you later.
Girl	Bye.

★★★ **5** Write a phone conversation between you and
a friend. Use your own names, place and time
and/or the ideas below.

- Bert / Maggie / movie theater / five thirty
- Ali / Josh / library / 1:30
- Nicky / John / park / three fifteen
- Sarah / Faith / mall / one forty

Speaking and Listening page 136

Grammar • Past simple: questions

★ 1 Read the questions and complete the answers.

1 Did you go to Lily's birthday party?
Yes, *I did.*
2 Did Lily have a birthday cake?
Yes, ...
3 Did Tom bring Lily a present?
Yes, ...
4 Did Lily's mom and dad dance?
No, ...
5 Did it rain?
No, ...
6 Did you and your friends enjoy the party?
Yes, ...

★ 2 Complete the questions.

Ryan Where ¹ *did* you *go* (go) yesterday?
Alice I went to the movies.
Ryan Who ² .... you .... (go) with?
Alice I went with my sister and two friends.
Ryan What ³ .... you .... (see)?
Alice We saw the last Harry Potter movie.
Ryan ⁴ .... you .... (enjoy) it?
Alice Yes. It was great!
Ryan What time ⁵ .... it .... (end)?
Alice It ended at ten o'clock.
Ryan How ⁶ .... you ....
(get) home?
Alice My mom picked us up and took us home.

★ 3 Write the questions for the answers with these question words.

| How | What | When | Where | Who | ~~Why~~ |

1 *Why did you leave?*
I left because I was cold.
2 ....
He met Lucy and Mark.
3 ....
They arrived at six thirty.
4 ....
She wore a blue coat and a purple scarf.
5 ....
I went to the supermarket.
6 ....
We traveled by bus.

Grammar Reference pages 124–125

★★ 4 Look at the card. Write the questions about the missing information.

Hi Louise,
I'm on vacation in Spain with my family. We arrived here last ¹ ●●. On Monday we went to the ² ●●. I loved it. We ate ³ ●● in an Italian restaurant in the evening. The next day we traveled by ⁴ ●● to Cordoba. I saw ⁵ ●● at the station! It's a small world! Enjoy your trip to Canada.
Love, Ben

1 When *did Ben and his family arrive in Spain?*
2 Where .... ?
3 What .... ?
4 How .... ?
5 Who .... ?

★★ 5 Match the questions in Exercise 4 to the answers.

a ☐ He saw his Spanish teacher.
b ☐ They traveled by train.
c ☑ They arrived last night.
d ☐ They went to the theater.
e ☐ They ate pasta and shrimp.

★★ 6 Look at the picture of Jane's shopping trip last week. Write questions and answers.

1 where / go → downtown
Where did Jane go?   She went downtown.
2 wear / hat / → yes
Did she wear a hat?
....
3 what / buy / → clothes
....
....
4 rain / → no
....
....

Reading

1 Read the quiz quickly. What means of transportation can you find?

boat, train, …

2 Take the quiz. Then listen and check your answers.
33

The Great Transportation Quiz

wheel

1 The 1519–1522 Spanish Expedition led by Ferdinand Magellan was the first to travel around the world. How did they travel?

a by boat   **b** by train   **c** by bus

2 The first underground railway in the world opened in 1863. Today it has 402 kilometers of track and is often called the Tube. Where is it?

a Paris   **b** Moscow   **c** London

3 On January 21, 1976, a supersonic plane carried about 100 passengers from London to Bahrain. It was faster than the speed of sound. What was the name of the plane?

a Atlantis   **b** Concorde   **c** Icarus

4 This American car, a limousine, is more than 30 meters long. It has 26 wheels, and you can drive the car from both ends. What's in the car?

a a swimming pool   **b** a disco   **c** a library

5 Harley-Davidson motorcycles are popular everywhere in the world. Many famous actors, including Brad Pitt and George Clooney, have a Harley-Davidson. Where do they come from?

a Japan   **b** the US   **c** Australia

6 *Murder on the Orient Express* is a book by Agatha Christie. The Orient Express traveled from Paris, France, to Istanbul, Turkey. What was it?

a a helicopter   **b** a bus   **c** a train

---

3 Now read about your score.

Your score?
0–2 Oh no! Find out about transportation.
3–4 Great! You know some interesting facts.
5–6 Awesome!

4 Read the quiz again. Answer the questions.

1 Where did the first expedition to travel around the world come from? *It came from Spain.*

2 When did the Tube open?

....

3 Where did the supersonic plane fly on January 21, 1976?

....

4 How long is the limousine?

....

5 What is a Harley-Davidson?

....

6 Where did the Orient Express begin and end its trip?

....

Listening

1 Listen. Mark what the family is talking about.
34
1 Going on vacation.   ☐
2 Watching TV shows.   ☐
3 Buying a new car.   ☐

2 Listen again. Are the statements true (T) or false (F)?
34
1 They want to go to Oregon.   *T*
2 They live near Oregon.   ....
3 Sally takes a lot of books on vacation..   ....
4 Paul doesn't want to go by bus.   ....
5 They are talking about a winter vacation.   ....

3 Listen again. Answer the questions.
34
1 Why don't they go by plane? *It's expensive.*
2 Why don't they go by car?

....

3 Why don't they go by train?

....

4 Why don't they go by bus?

....

5 What does Mom suggest they do?

....

Writing • A travel diary

1 Read Karen's diary. Mark the correct statement (the paragraphs are not in order).

1 The paragraphs describe different sports. ☐
2 The paragraphs describe different times of the day. ☐
3 The paragraphs describe different places. ☐

a This evening we watched a funny movie in the theater. I'm writing this in bed. I'm sharing a bedroom with Patsy and Rosa. I must go to sleep now because there are a lot of activities tomorrow. I'm really excited because they look super fun!

b Today was the first day of our school trip to the Lakeside Adventure Center. The bus left from the school parking lot at eight thirty this morning. I sat next to Rosa. First, we ate the sandwiches from our packed lunch. Later we talked to the boys in the seat behind us. Then we ate everything else in our packed lunches. At twelve thirty the bus stopped for lunch, but we didn't have anything left!

c We arrived at two thirty. In the afternoon, we walked around the lake. Later we had dinner in the big hall.

2 Read the diary again. Number the paragraphs in order.

1 ....   2 ....   3 ....

3 Read the diary again. Answer the questions.

1 Where is the trip to?
The trip is to the Lakeside Adventure Center.
2 When did the trip start?
....
3 How did they travel?
....
4 What did they do in the afternoon?
....
5 What did they do in the evening?
....
6 Who is sleeping in the same room as Karen?
....

Brain Trainer

Before you plan your writing, think of as many ideas as you can and write them in a mind map.
Add two ideas to each mind map.

beach   lake
Places to visit
....

go sailing   go swimming
Things to do
....

Now do Exercise 4.

4 Take notes about your own school trip. Use the questions in Exercise 3.

Paragraph 1
1 ....
2 ....
3 ....

Paragraph 2
4 ....
5 ....

Paragraph 3
6 ....
7 ....

5 Write a short diary about the first day of your school trip. Use the model in Exercise 1 and your notes from Exercise 4.

....
....
....
....
....
....
....
....
....
....
....
....
....
....

9 Technology Time

Vocabulary • Technology

★ **1** **Choose seven items of technology that you can touch.**

broadband   social networking sites

Wi-Fi

blog

netbook

screen

smart phone

flash drive   instant messaging

digital radio

e-reader

interactive whiteboard

★ **2** **Write the words from Exercise 1 next to the correct object.**

1 *digital radio*   2 ....   3 ....

4 ....   5 ....

6 ....   7 ....

★ **3** **Complete the conversation. Use the words you didn't choose in Exercise 1.**

Dad   What are you doing?

Sarah   I'm trying to find Justin Bieber's ¹ *blog*. I want to know everything he does. The computer's really slow today. Why don't we have ² .... ?

Dad   We're getting it on Saturday. We're getting ³ .... too, so you can use your laptop in every room in the house.

Dad   I thought you were on Justin's website.

Sarah   No. I'm chatting with friends now.

Dad   You spend too much time on ⁴ ....

Sarah   I love them. The ⁵ .... is awesome. I can talk to all my friends at the same time.

Dad   You spend all day with your friends at school.

Sarah   But Dad, that's different!

★★ **4** **Choose the correct options.**

1 You want to read a novel. You can use …
   a instant messaging   b a digital radio
   c an e-reader

2 You want to talk to your friends. You can use …
   a instant messaging   b a flash drive
   c an interactive whiteboard

3 You want to take the homework you did on your computer to school. You can use …
   a Wi-Fi   b a screen   c a flash drive

4 You want to take a photo of your friends. You can use …
   a an e-reader   b a smart phone   c a blog

5 You want to listen to music. You can use …
   a a social networking site
   b a digital radio   c a screen

6 You want to write and tell people about what happens at school. You can use …
   a a blog   b broadband   c an e-reader

★★ **5** **Answer the questions.**

1 What technology do you use at home?
....

2 What technology do you use at your school?
....

3 Who do you know that writes a blog?
....

4 What social networking sites do you use?
....

5 What can you do with a smart phone?
....

Workbook page 132

Reading

★ **1** Read the advertisements quickly. Match the names (1–3) to the technology words (a–c).

1 The Candy 3G is   a a digital radio.
2 The Sung S2 is   b an e-reader.
3 The Albert 35 is   c a netbook.

★ **2** Read the advertisements again. Label the photos.

1 ....

2 ....

3 ....

★★ **3** Look at the advertisements again. Write Candy 3G (C), Sung S2 (S) or Albert 35 (A).

1 It has Wi-Fi.   S
2 You can choose its color.   ....
3 You can read novels on it.   ....
4 It's cheaper than the digital radio.   ....
5 You can watch movies on it.   ....
6 It doesn't have a screen.   ....

★★★ **4** Answer the questions.

1 How many books can you store on the Candy 3G?

....

2 How much is the Candy?

....

3 How big is the netbook screen?

....

4 How much is the Sung S2?

....

5 Where is the best place for the digital radio?

....

6 How many colors can you choose from?

....

1

Sam's going to take her new Candy 3G on vacation. Why?

I want to go to the beach and read every day, but I don't want to take a lot of books. I'm going to take my Candy 3G because it's light, and I can carry it in my bag. It has all the books I want to read on it.

In fact, it stores up to 3,500 books, and it's only $150!

Buy the Sung S2, and you're going to love it! It's light, it's fast, and it's easy to use—and it has a 25 cm screen! You get Wi-Fi too, so you can go online wherever you are. Find your favorite websites. Enjoy chatting with friends. Watch movies and TV shows. Send emails. Play games. At $400, it's a winner!

3

The Albert 35 is just what you need next to your bed. Set your alarm for the morning, and you can wake up to your favorite music. And with the Albert 35, you can listen to your favorite shows at any time. It's also a CD player, and it can play from an MP3 player or a flash drive. It's available in red, black or white and costs $349!

Grammar • Be going to

★⃝1 **Choose the correct options.**

1 They *isn't / aren't* going to work this evening.
2 *I'm going to / I'm going* take the bus.
3 Is he *go to / going to* close the door?
   Yes, *he is going to / he is*.
4 *Are you / Is you* going to listen to your new CD?
   No, *I'm not / I'm not going*.
5 *It not / It isn't* going to rain.
6 *We going to calling / We're going to call*
   our cousins.

★⃝2 **Complete the sentences with the correct form of**
***be going to* and the verb.**

1 They*'re going to watch* (watch) a DVD tonight.
2 I .... (buy) a smart phone
   next month.
3 He .... (wear) his new
   shoes tomorrow.
4 She .... (not play) the guitar.
5 They .... (not go) bowling.
6 We .... (visit) the technology
   fair next week.

★★⃝3 **Look at the picture. Complete the sentences with**
***is/isn't/are/aren't going to* and the correct verb.**

| buy | ~~meet~~ | play | stop | wear |

1 The girls *are going to meet* their friend.
2 The bus ....
3 The children .... tennis.
4 The man .... a newspaper.
5 The police officer .... his cap.

★★⃝4 **Look at the picture in Exercise 3. Complete the**
questions with *Is* or *Are* . Then answer the questions.

1 *Are* the girls going to go into the café?
   Yes, they are.
2 .... the woman going to get on the bus?
   ....
3 .... the children going to cross the street?
   ....
4 .... the man going to walk home?
   ....
5 .... the police officer going to drive the car?
   ....
6 .... it going to rain?
   ....

★★⃝5 **What are you going to do this evening? Mark**
(✓ or ✗) the activities. Then write true sentences.

My plans for this evening
1 do my homework
2 have dinner with my family
3 clean up my room
4 watch TV
5 go on a social networking site
6 go to bed early

1 *I'm going to do my homework./I'm not going*
   to do my homework.
2 ....
3 ....
4 ....
5 ....
6 ....

Grammar Reference pages 126–127

⃝110 Unit 9 • Technology Time

Vocabulary • Technology phrases

★(1) Choose the correct options.

1 use the (Internet) / interactive
2 charge a search engine / a phone
3 download a phone / videos and movies
4 write a blog / Wi-Fi
5 go movies / online
6 send emails / online
7 use a text / Wi-Fi

★(2) Put the letters in the correct order.

1 esdn a xtte   send a text
2 ues a erscha genein   ....
3 acth nloien   ....
4 rhaecg a npohe   ....
5 riewt a olbg   ....
6 londowad umics   ....

★(3) Look at the pictures. Complete the sentences with these phrases.

charging a phone   chatting online
~~downloading music~~   sending a text
writing a blog

1 She's *downloading music*.
2 He's ....
3 He's ....
4 He's ....
5 She's ....

Brain Trainer

Words you know can be used in new contexts.
Read the text in Exercise 4 and find what else you can download.

download music/movies/videos/ …

Now do Exercise 4.

★★(4) Choose the correct options.

We love technology in my family. My dad works from home, so we have [1] (Wi-Fi) / flash drive and a super fast [2] broadband / text connection. My older sister [3] sends / goes online when she gets home from school. She likes [4] chatting / using with her friends online. My mom has a new [5] smart phone / instant messaging. She [6] writes / uses it all the time. She likes it because it does a lot of things. She can call people and take photos, and she can [7] download / know her emails wherever she is. Actually, she isn't using it at the moment because it needs [8] emailing / charging.

★★(5) Complete the sentences with these words. Then match the descriptions to the technology (a–e) below.

charge   chat   downloading   send   ~~use~~

1 Teachers *use* this in the classroom.   b
2 You must .... this before you take it to the beach to read your new book.   ....
3 You can call your friends, take photos and .... texts and emails with this.   ....
4 I'm .... the new movie so I can watch it tonight. Then I'm going to write about it tomorrow.   ....
5 You can .... online with your friends when you join this.   ....

a blog
b interactive whiteboard
c social networking site
d smart phone
e e-reader

Workbook page 132

Speaking and Listening

★ 1 **Match the statements (1–4) to the sentences asking for more information (a–d).**

1 I missed math this morning.   *b*
2 There's a movie on tonight.
  Do you want to watch it?   ....
3 I'm having a bad day.   ....
4 I'm leaving school in July.   ....

a Why? Tell me about it.
b Why? What happened?
c Oh. What are you planning?
d What is it about? Can you tell me more?

★ 2 **Listen and read the conversation. <u>Underline</u>**
35 **the phrases asking for information.**

Frank	Beth, I'm writing about school clubs for the school newsletter. <u>Can you tell me about</u> the drama club?
Beth	Yes, of course. We put on a play or musical every summer, although we didn't do one last year.
Frank	Why not? What happened?
Beth	Miss Laws, the drama teacher, was out sick that semester.
Frank	What are you doing this year?
Beth	We're doing *Romeo and Juliet.*
Frank	Tell me about it.
Beth	It's a sad love story.
Frank	What are you planning for next year?
Beth	Next summer we're going to do a musical, but I don't know which one.
Frank	OK. That's great. Thanks for your help, Beth.

★★ 3 **Read the conversation again. Answer the questions.**

1 Why does Frank want to know about the drama club?
  He's writing about school clubs for the school newsletter.
2 Why wasn't there a school play last year?
  ....
3 What is the drama club going to do next year?
  ....

Speaking and Listening page 137

Brain Trainer

Guess the meaning of a new word from the context. Read the dialogue in Exercise 4 and find the word *detention*. What do you think it means?

a a free lesson
b extra time at school for being late, not doing homework, shouting in class and the like
c a box of chocolates

Look it up in a dictionary. Then do Exercise 4.

★★ 4 **Complete the conversation with these phrases.**
36 **Then listen and check.**

~~Tell me about it.~~
What are you planning for the weekend?
What did you do?
What happened?

Dan	I'm having a bad week.
Stacey	Oh. ¹ *Tell me about it.*
Dan	On Thursday I had detention.
Stacey	Why? ² ....
Dan	I was late to school.
Stacey	Bad luck.
Dan	And yesterday I needed to go to the hospital.
Stacey	Really? ³ ....
Dan	I fell off my bike. I'm glad it's Saturday tomorrow.
Stacey	⁴ ....
Dan	I'm getting up late, and I'm staying at home. I don't want another bad day!

★★ 5 **Write a conversation between you and a friend about the week. Use the model in Exercise 4 and the ideas below to help you.**

On Thursday
  have extra homework / not pass the exam
  my best friend have a fight with me / eat all her candy
Yesterday
  late to school / miss the bus
  lose my bag / leave it in a café
On the Weekend
  get up early / go to the swimming pool
  go to the mall / buy a new coat

Grammar • Present continuous for future arrangements

★ **1** Choose the correct options.

1 *Are they going* / *Are they go* to the party on Saturday?
2 She *'s staying* / *stays* at home tomorrow.
3 They *'s visiting* / *'re visiting* their grandparents next month.
4 What *does he wear* / *is he wearing* tonight?
5 I *'m not coming* / *don't coming* to school next week.
6 *Is the train leaving* / *Are the train leave* at 10:05?

★ **2** Complete the sentences with the correct form of the Present continuous.

1 Jon *'s meeting* (meet) Helen at 4 p.m.
2 The school .... (not close) early on Friday.
3 I .... (go) to the movies tonight.
4 They .... (fly) to New York next week.
5 **A** .... you .... (wear) your new pants tomorrow?
  B No, I ....
6 We .... (not play) in the tournament next weekend.
7 I .... (not go shopping) on Saturday.
8 **A** .... she .... (have) a birthday party this summer?
  B Yes, she ....

★ **3** Look at Tammy's planner for next week. Write the questions.

Monday	write to
Tuesday	meet Sam at
Wednesday	watch the
Thursday	go to the
Friday	play basketball at
Saturday	buy a present for

1 Who *is Tammy writing to on Monday?*
2 When .... ?
3 What .... ?
4 Where .... ?
5 What time .... ?
6 Who .... ?

★★ **4** Look at the missing part of Tammy's planner. Answer the questions in Exercise 3.

Dev.
4:30
school play
doctor's office
5:15
Luke

1 *She's writing to Dev.*
2 ....
3 ....
4 ....
5 ....
6 ....

★★ **5** Look at the pictures. Write sentences about Nick's vacation next week. Use these words and phrases.

~~fly / LA, California~~	go concert / park
horseback ride / mountains	surf / beach
visit wax museum / Hollywood	

Nick

Day 1 *Nick's flying to LA, California.*
Day 2 ....
Day 3 ....
Day 4 ....
Day 5 ....

Grammar Reference pages 126–127

Reading

1 Quickly read the page from a school textbook. Choose the best title.

1 The History of Technology
2 The Invention of Television
3 The History of Telephones

Today, people spend about seven hours every day using technology such as television, radios, MP3 players, phones and computers. Teenagers spend a lot of this time using their cell phones. Alexander Graham Bell invented the first telephone in the UK in 1876, but it was only in 1973 that Dr. Martin Cooper at Motorola invented the cell phone in the US. The phones were very big and heavy, and they were unpopular because there weren't any networks. Japan created the first network in 1979. The first cell phones only made phone calls—they didn't do anything else. Then, in 1993, people started sending text messages in Finland, and cell phones became more popular. Today, 85 percent of American adults have a cell phone, and half of British teenagers have smart phones.

Smart phones are cell phones, but you can do a lot more than make phone calls with them. You can send texts, take photos and videos, listen to the radio and connect to the Internet. When you are online, you can watch movies, send emails, play games … and much more. In the future, smart phones are going to get thinner, like paper, and they are going to get even smarter!

2 Read the page again. Complete the information.

	Country	Year
Alexander Graham Bell invented the first telephone.	¹ UK	1876
Dr. Martin Cooper invented the cell phone.	2	
The first cellular network started.	3	
People sent text messages.	4	

3 Answer the questions.

1 How long do people spend using technology every day?
They spend about seven hours using technology.
2 Why didn't many people have cell phones in 1973?
....
3 How many Americans have cell phones now?
....
4 How many British teenagers have smart phones?
....
5 What can you do with a smart phone connected to the Internet?
....
6 How are smart phones going to change?
....

Listening

1 Listen to a quiz about technology. Choose the correct options.
37

1 Who invented *television* / *the telephone*?
2 What's an *IM* / *IWB*?
3 What technology can you use to read *novels* / *emails*?
4 What does *LOL* / *WWW* stand for?
5 What are *Twitter and Facebook* / *broadband and Wi-Fi*?
6 Where does *Bill Gates* / *solar power* come from?

2 Write the answers to the questions in Exercise 1. Then listen again and check.
37

1 *John Logie Baird.*
2 ....
3 ....
4 ....
5 ....
6 ....

Writing • A story

1 Complete the Writing File Review with these words.

> because   commas   group
> paragraphs   ~~punctuation~~

Writing File Review
Remember to use all your writing skills!

a Check your [1] *punctuation*
   Do you have periods, capital letters,
   [2] .... , question marks
   and exclamation points?
b Use linking words
   Use *and*, *but* or [3] ....
   to join phrases or words in a sentence.
c Write in [4] ....
   Is the information in a [5] .... ?

2 Read the story. Circle the punctuation and underline the linking words.

Last week I dropped my cell phone on the way to school. I looked everywhere for it, but I didn't find it. My mom was very angry with me when I got home.

Yesterday a strange thing happened. My friends got a text from LeBron James. He's my favorite basketball player, and he found my phone!

I'm so happy today. I have my phone back, and LeBron sent me two tickets for the next Cleveland Cavaliers game! I'm going, with my dad, to watch them play Miami Heat next month. Can you believe it?

Darren

3 Read the story again. Are the statements true (T) or false (F)?

1 There are four paragraphs.   *F*
2 Paragraph 1 describes what happened
   at the beginning of the story.   ....
3 Paragraph 2 describes what happened
   last month.   ....
4 Paragraph 3 describes the end of the story.   ....
5 The story has a happy ending.   ....

4 Read the story again. Correct the sentences.

1 Darren lost his phone yesterday.
   Darren lost his phone last week.
2 His mom was angry because he got home late.
   ....
   ....
3 LeBron James sent a photo to Darren's friends.
   ....
   ....
4 Darren sent LeBron two tickets.
   ....
   ....
5 Cleveland Cavaliers are going to play Miami
   Heat today.
   ....
   ....

5 You are going to write a story. Take notes and plan your story. Use these ideas to help you.

The object
netbook / smart phone / flash drive / e-reader

The finder
famous person / someone in your family /
an alien / an animal

Think of a title for your story.

• **Paragraph 1**
  What did you lose?
  Where and when did you lose it?

• **Paragraph 2**
  Who found it?
  How did he/she contact you?

• **Paragraph 3**
  What did the person who found your
  object do?
  What is going to happen?

6 Now write your story. Use the model in Exercise 2 and your notes from Exercise 5.

....
....
....
....
....
....
....
....

Check 3

Grammar

1 Complete the text with the Past simple of the verbs.

Yesterday ⁰ *was* (be) great! I ¹ .... (go) to New York for the first time. We ² .... (take) the 9:10 train and ³ .... (arrive) two hours later. First, we ⁴ .... (visit) the Empire State Building. We ⁵ .... (not eat) at the café there. We ⁶ .... (have) some sandwiches in a park. Then we ⁷ .... (see) the musical *Aladdin*—it ⁸ .... (be) fantastic! We ⁹ .... (get) home late. I ¹⁰ .... (not go) to bed until 1 a.m!

/ 5 points

2 Look at the picture. Write questions and answers.

0 Rachel and her family / go / to New York
Did Rachel and her family go to New York?
Yes, they did.
1 they / have lunch / outside
....
....
2 they / wear / coats
....
....
3 Rachel's mom / take / any photos
....
....
4 there / be / any cars in the park
....
....
5 there / be / many people in the park
....
....

/ 5 points

3 Write what the people are going to do.

0 talk / teacher ✘   talk / her friend ✔
She isn't going to talk to the teacher.
She's going to talk to her friend.
1 buy / digital radio ✔   buy / netbook ✘
They ....
They ....
2 travel / train ✘   travel / bus ✔
I ....
I ....
3 wear / sneakers ✔   wear sandals ✘
We ....
We ....
4 download / music ✘   download / a movie ✔
He ....
He ....

/ 8 points

4 Look at Rob's planner. What is he doing next week?

Rob's planner

Monday	see Mr. Woods about math homework
Tuesday	visit grandpa after school
Wednesday	go to the doctor
Thursday	have extra English class at lunchtime
Friday	evening—watch World Cup at George's house
Saturday	play soccer game against Charlston

0 *On Monday he's seeing Mr. Woods about his math homework.*
1 ....
2 ....
3 ....
4 ....
5 ....

/ 5 points

Vocabulary

5 Complete the text with the correct transportation. Then write the date next to each picture.

When I was five, in 1992, I got my first ⁰ b*ike*. In 2002 I got my first vehicle. It was a motor ¹ s_ _ _ _ _ _. I went to school on it. Two years later, my dad gave me my first ² c_ _. When I started my job in 2007, I bought a white ³ v_ _. I learned to drive a ⁴ t_ _ _ _ four years later. Next year I'm going to buy a ⁵ b_ _ so I can take all my friends on a trip.

0 *1992*   1 ....

2 ....   3 ....

4 ....   5 ....

/ 5 points

6 Circle the word that doesn't fit. Then match the uncircled words to the categories (a–e).

0 chat   charge   download   (study)   0
1 subway   blog   train   boat
2 sneakers   e-book   smart phone   Wi-Fi
3 third   sail   first   fourth
4 helicopter   ask   travel   close
5 scarf   hat   second   coat

0 technology verbs
a clothes
b verbs
c transportation
d ordinal numbers
e technology

/ 5 points

Speaking

7 Choose the incorrect sentences.

0 a I went shopping two days ago.
  b I went shopping last week.
  (c) I went shopping for two years.
1 a We moved here in the 1990s.
  b We moved here more than twenty years ago.
  c We moved here next month.
2 a The dog was in the backyard ten minutes ago.
  b The dog was in the backyard tomorrow.
  c The dog was in the backyard this morning.
3 a I wasn't very well last week.
  b I wasn't very well yesterday.
  c I wasn't very well soon.
4 a We stayed there for a week ago.
  b We stayed there for the weekend.
  c We stayed there for two weeks.

/ 4 points

Translation

8 Translate the sentences.

1 My dad's going to buy a smart phone next week.
....

2 We didn't fly in a plane; we went by helicopter.
....

3 I'm going to charge my phone tonight.
....

4 There weren't any netbooks in the 1980s.
....

5 The girl wore a blue dress and brown sandals.
....

6 I did all my homework this week.
....

7 He wore black pants and white sneakers.
....

8 My dad takes the subway to work.
....

/ 8 points

Dictation

9 Listen and write.
38

/ 5 points

Grammar Reference

• Present continuous

Affirmative		
I	'm (am)	reading.
He/She/It	is	reading.
You/We/They	're (are)	reading.
Negative		
I	'm not (am not)	playing.
He/She/It	isn't (is not)	playing.
You/We/They	aren't (are not)	playing.
Questions and short answers		
Am I singing?	Yes, I am. / No, I'm not.	
Is he/she/it singing?	Yes, he/she/it is. No, he/she/it isn't.	
Are you/we/they singing?	Yes, you/we/they are. No, you/we/they aren't.	
Wh questions		
What are you watching?		

Time expressions

(right) now
today
at the moment

Use

- We use the Present continuous to talk about actions that are happening now.
  She's *playing* the guitar at the moment.

Form

- We form the Present continuous with *to be* (*am, is* or *are*) + main verb + **-ing**.
  They're *making* a cake.

- To form the negative, we add *not* after *am, is* or *are*.
  The dog *isn't swimming* in the ocean. (= is not)

- The word order changes in questions: *Am/Is/Are* + subject + main verb + **-ing**.
  Are you *painting* a picture of your sister?

- In short answers, we do not repeat the main verb.
  A Is he *climbing* that mountain?   **B** Yes, he *is*.

• Spelling rules: verb + -ing

most verbs: add **-ing**	play → playing
verbs that end in **-e**: drop the **-e** and add **-ing**	come → coming
verbs that end in one vowel + one consonant: double the consonant and add **-ing**	sit → sitting

Common mistakes

He's dancing. ✓
He dancing. ✗
Are they talking? ✓
They are talking? ✗
We're watching a movie. ✓
We're watch a movie. ✗

• Present simple and Present continuous

Present simple	Present continuous
I often swim here.	I'm looking at the animals now.

Use
Present simple

We use the Present simple to talk about:

- routines and habits.
  I *go* to the movies every weekend.

- things that are true in general.
  Goats *live* in the mountains.

- Time expressions:
  adverbs of frequency (*never, hardly ever, sometimes, usually/often, always*), *every day/week/month, every Saturday, on the weekend, after school, on Wednesday at two o'clock*

Present continuous

- We use the Present continuous to talk about things that are happening now.
  She's *watching* her favorite TV show at the moment.

- Time expressions: *now, today, at the moment*

Common mistake

I usually do gymnastics on Mondays, but today I'm playing basketball. ✓

I usually am doing gymnastics but today I play basketball. ✗

Grammar practice • Present continuous

1 Complete the table with the *-ing* form of these verbs.

drink	get	go	have	jump	make
run	sit	swim	take	watch	write

+ -ing	e + -ing	x2 + -ing
drinking	having	getting
....	....	....
....	....	....
....	....	....

2 Look at the picture. Complete the sentences with these verbs. Then write the names on the picture.

drive	eat	snow	take	talk	wear

1 It *'s snowing* in the mountains.
2 Becky .... a photo.
3 Oliver .... his car.
4 Becky and I .... warm clothes.
5 Bill and Amanda .... lunch.
6 I .... on my cell phone.

3 Complete the conversation with the Present continuous of the verbs.

Dad What ¹ *are you reading* (you / read)?
Fred I ² .... (not read).
I ³ .... (look) for a word in this dictionary.
Dad What subject ⁴ ....
(you / study)?
Fred I ⁵ .... (study) English right now. We ⁶ ....
(learn) the words for different outdoor activities, and I ⁷ ....
(write) about my favorite activities.

4 Complete the questions. Then match the questions (1–5) to the answers (a–e).

1 What *are you doing* (you / do)?   d
2 Where .... (you / go)?
3 Who .... (you / sit) next to?
4 Why .... (they / open) the window?
5 When .... (we / arrive)?

a To New Haven.
b At 4:15.
c Because it's hot.
d I'm sitting on a train.
e My sister.

• Present simple and Present continuous

5 Rewrite the sentences using the correct time expression.

1 We're playing baseball. (every week / now)
We're playing baseball now.
2 The children go kayaking. (usually / at the moment)
....
3 She isn't swimming in the ocean. (never / at the moment)
....
4 I'm taking the dog for a walk. (today / every day)
....
5 You don't sing in the shower. (tonight / often)
....

6 Complete the sentences and questions. Use the Present simple or Present continuous.

1 I *'m not watching* (not watch) TV at the moment.
2 Dr. Barrett .... (go) to the hospital every morning.
3 .... (it / rain) now?
4 They .... (not get up) early on the weekend.
5 .... (she / swim) in the ocean in the summer?
6 Who .... (we / wait) for?

Grammar Reference

• Countable and uncountable nouns

Countable nouns		Uncountable nouns
Singular	**Plural**	some bread
a sandwich	some sandwiches	some pasta
a tomato	some tomatoes	some rice
an apple	some apples	some water

Form

- Countable nouns can be singular or plural.
  egg → eggs   vegetable → vegetables

- Uncountable nouns have no plural form.
  juice, pasta, water

- We use *a* before singular countable nouns starting with a consonant sound.
  a potato, a sandwich

- We use *an* before singular countable nouns starting with a vowel sound.
  an apple, an orange

- We can use *some* before plural countable nouns and uncountable nouns.
  some tomatoes, some chicken

• Many/Much/A lot of

How many?	How much?
How many bananas do you have?	How much yogurt do you have?
We don't have any bananas.	We don't have any yogurt.
We don't have many bananas.	We don't have much yogurt.
We have some/four bananas.	We have some yogurt.
We have a lot of bananas.	We have a lot of yogurt.

Use

- We can use *many, some* and *a lot of* with countable nouns.
  many apples, some apples, a lot of apples

- We can use *much, some* and *a lot of* with uncountable nouns.
  much pasta, some pasta, a lot of pasta

- We use *How much?* and *How many?* to ask about quantities.
  How much water is there?
  How many friends do you have?

- We usually use *a lot of* in affirmative sentences.
  There are a lot of books on the table.

- We usually use *much* and *many* in negative sentences and questions.
  There isn't much juice.
  Do you have many pets?

• Comparatives

Short adjectives	Comparatives
old	older (than)
hot	hotter (than)
nice	nicer (than)
happy	happier (than)
Long adjectives	**Comparatives**
popular	more popular (than)
interesting	more interesting (than)
Irregular adjectives	**Comparatives**
good	better (than)
bad	worse (than)

Use

- We use comparative adjectives to compare two people or things.
  *The café is **cheaper** than the restaurant.*

Form

Short adjectives	Comparatives
most adjectives: add **-er**	small → smaller
adjectives that end in **-e**: add **-r**	nice → nicer
adjectives that end in one vowel + one consonant: double the consonant and add **-er**	hot → hotter
adjectives that end in **-y**: drop the **y** and add **-ier**	pretty → prettier
Long adjectives	
add **more**	interesting → more interesting
irregular adjectives	good → better
bad → worse

Grammar practice • Countable and uncountable nouns

1 Write Countable (C) or Uncountable (U).

1	time	*U*	6 watches	*C*
2	butter	....	7 eggs	....
3	lake	....	8 water	....
4	wallet	....	9 money	....
5	music	....	10 songs	....

• Many/Much/A lot of

2 Complete the questions with *How much* or *How many*.

1 *How much* bread do we have?
2 .... bananas are there?
3 .... rice is there?
4 .... apples do we have?
5 .... eggs do we need?
6 .... milk is in the fridge?

3 Look at the picture and the table. Write sentences.

There	's isn't are aren't	a lot of much many	cheese sandwiches fruit sausage juice chips

1 *There isn't much cheese.*
2 ....
3 ....
4 ....
5 ....
6 ....

• Comparatives

4 Choose the correct options. Then match the sentences (1–5) to the rules (a–e) and write the base adjective.

1 Debbie's (thinner) / thiner than Rodney.   *c*
2 Laura's *happyer* / *happier* than Katie.
3 Peter's *interestingger* / *more interesting* than James.
4 Paul's *taller* / *tallr* than Yvonne.
5 Jane's *nicer* / *more nice* than her sister.

a *more* + long adjective   ....
b + *-er*   ....
c x2 + *-er*   *thin*
d + *-r*   ....
e *-y* + *-ier*   ....

5 Look at the pictures. Complete the sentences.

A

B

1 **old**
   The man in B *is older than the man in A.*
2 **hot**
   The cup of coffee in B ....
3 **thin**
   The woman in B ....
4 **large**
   The salad in B ....
5 **dirty**
   The boy in B ....

Grammar Reference

Past simple: *to be*

Affirmative		
I/He/She/It	was	in the library.
You/We/They	were	in the library.
Negative		
I/He/She/It	wasn't (was not)	in the backyard.
You/We/They	weren't (were not)	in the backyard.
Questions and short answers		
Was I/he/she/it noisy?	Yes, I/he/she/it was. / No, I/he/she/it wasn't (was not).	
Were you/we/they dirty?	Yes, you/we/they were. / No, you/we/they weren't (were not).	

Time expressions

yesterday   a week ago   yesterday morning
in 1845   last month

Use

- We use the Past simple to talk about states (or actions) that began and finished in the past.
  *They **were** at home yesterday.*

Form

- To form the affirmative, we use subject + *was/were*.
  *I **was** at the library.*   *We **were** on the train.*
- To form the negative, we add *not* after *was/were*.
  *It **wasn't** very expensive. (= was not)*
- The word order changes in questions: *Was/Were* + subject.
  __Was__ he happy?   *__Were__ they late?*

There was/There were

Affirmative	
There was a movie/some juice.	
There were some comics.	
Negative	
There wasn't a museum/any coffee.	
There weren't any magazines.	
Questions and short answers	
Was there a bus station/any tea?	Yes, there was.
Were there any books?	No, there weren't.

Use

- We use *there was/were* to say something existed or didn't exist in the past.
  __There was__ color TV twenty years ago.
  __There weren't__ any interactive whiteboards in 1990.
- We use *there was* and *there wasn't* with singular and uncountable nouns.
  __There was__ a movie theater in the shopping mall.
  __There wasn't__ any pasta in the store.
- We use *there were/weren't* with plural nouns.
  __There were__ some good shows on TV last week.
  __There weren't__ many cars on our street fifty years ago.

Form

- To form the affirmative, we use *there* + *was/were*.
  __There was__ a poster of the Beatles on his wall.
  __There were__ some famous models in the 1960s.
- To form the negative, we add *not* after *was/were*.
  *There **wasn't** a phone booth near our house.*
  *There **weren't** any cell phones in the 1960s.*
- To form questions, we use *Was/Were* + *there*.
  __Was__ there a school trip to New Orleans last year?
  __Were__ there any DVDs five years ago?

Past simple: regular affirmative and negative

Affirmative		
I/You/He/She/It/We/They	lived	in an old house.
Negative		
I/You/He/She/It/We/They	didn't (did not) live	in an old house.

Use

- We use the Past simple to talk about states or actions that began and finished in the past.
  *She **listened** to the radio.*

Form

- To form the Past simple of regular verbs, we add **-ed**, **-d** or **-ied** to the verb. (See Spelling rules.)
  *He **asked** questions about the 1950s.*
- To form the negative of regular verbs, we use *didn't (did not)* + the main verb in the infinitive.
  *She **didn't answer** the phone.*

• We use time expressions to say <u>when</u> we did something. The time expression goes at the beginning or at the end of the sentence.
*They traveled to Texas **last night**.*
__In the 1870s__, Mr. Bell invented the telephone.

• Spelling rules: verb + -ed

most verbs: add **-ed**	jump → jumped visit → visited
verbs that end in **-e**: add **-d**	live → lived die → died
verbs that end in consonant + **-y**: drop the **y** and add **-ied**	carry → carried study → studied
verbs that end in one vowel + one consonant: double the consonant and add **-ed**	drop → dropped

Grammar practice • Past simple: *to be*

1 **Complete the conversation with *was, wasn't, were* or *weren't*.**

Anna Where ¹ *were* you yesterday?
You ² .... at home.

Rosie No, I ³ .... I ⁴ ....
at Mario's, the Italian restaurant we like,
because it ⁵ .... my dad's birthday.

Anna How ⁶ .... it?

Rosie The food ⁷ .... delicious, but
the waiter ⁸ .... great.
⁹ .... you and Daisy at Carol's?

Anna No, we ¹⁰ .... Carol
¹¹ .... at her grandpa's house,
and Daisy and I ¹² .... at home.
Friends ¹³ .... on TV last night,
so we watched that.

• There was/There were

2 **Look at the shopping list and the basket, and write what was in the grocery store. Use *There was/wasn't, There were/weren't*.**

eggs	1 *There weren't any eggs.*
bananas	2 ....
chocolate	3 ....
magazine	4 ....
water	5 ....

3 **Look at the picture of Nina's grandma fifty years ago. Complete Nina's questions using *Was there/ Were there*. Write her grandma's answers.**

1 *Was there* a telephone in the house?
Yes, there was.

2 .... any DVDs?
....

3 .... any books or magazines?
....

4 .... a game console?
....

• Past simple regular: affirmative and negative

4 **Complete the table with the Past simple of these verbs.**

carry	chop	~~close~~	~~cook~~	dance	drop
like	listen	start	~~stop~~	~~study~~	try

+ -ed	x2 + -ed	+ -d	-y + -ied
cooked	stopped	closed	studied
....	....	....	....
....	....	....	....

5 **Complete the sentences with the Past simple of the verbs. Write one affirmative and one negative sentence.**

1 visit
We *didn't visit* the museum yesterday.
We *visited* our grandparents in the evening.

2 study
He .... French last year
because he wants to live in France.
Jessica .... literature because
she doesn't like reading.

3 stop
The bus .... near my house,
so I got home late again.
It .... next to the park.

Grammar Reference

• Past simple irregular: affirmative and negative

Affirmative		
I/You/He/She/It/We/They	had	breakfast.
Negative		
I/You/He/She/It/We/They	didn't (did not) have	breakfast.

Time expressions

yesterday	yesterday morning	last month
a week ago	in 1845	

Use

- We use the Past simple to talk about states or actions that began and finished in the past.
  *They **flew** to the US.*
  *He **didn't understand** the question.*

Form

- We don't add **-s** to the third person (**he/she/it**) in the Past simple.
  *He **did** his homework.*

- To form the negative of irregular verbs, we use *did not (didn't)* + the main verb in the infinitive.
  *We **didn't go** to school yesterday.*

- We use time expressions to say <u>when</u> we did something.
  *She bought a new car **last weekend**.*

- The time expression goes at the beginning or the end of the sentence.
  *Peter ran a marathon **two years ago**.*
  ***Two years ago**, Peter ran a marathon.*

• Past simple: questions

Regular verbs	
Did I/you/he/she/it/we/they visit the museum?	Yes, I/you/he/she/it/we/they did. No, I/you/he/she/it/we/they didn't.
Irregular verbs	
Did I/you/he/she/it/we/they see the Eiffel Tower?	Yes, I/you/he/she/it/we/they did. No, I/you/he/she/it/we/they didn't.
***Wh* questions**	
How did you travel? What did they do?	

Form

- To form questions, we use *Did* + the main verb in the infinitive. The word order also changes:
  Did + subject + main verb.
  ***Did** they **sail** to Spain?*
  ***Did** she **lose** her ticket?*

- In short answers, we do not repeat the main verb.
  A *Did you **enjoy** the movie?*   **B** *Yes, I **did**.*

Common mistake

Did they like the movie? ✓
~~*Did they liked the movie?*~~ ✗

Grammar practice • Past simple irregular: affirmative and negative

1 **Complete the sentences with the Past simple of these verbs.**

> drink   get up   go   have   ~~understand~~

1 I *understood* the question.
2 She .... at seven thirty yesterday.
3 We .... lunch at one thirty in the café in the town square.
4 They .... to the Empire State Building.
5 He .... two bottles of water because he was thirsty.

2 **Rewrite the text in the Past simple.**

Every year we ¹ **go** to the beach in the summer, and we ² **take** our dog, Trixie. We ³ **put** her in the back of the car. My mom ⁴ **drives,** and my dad ⁵ **reads** the map and ⁶ **tells** her where to go. We ⁷ **have** lunch on the way there. We ⁸ **eat** the picnic lunch that Mom ⁹ **makes** for the trip. It ¹⁰ **'s** a long trip, and we ¹¹ **are** happy when we ¹² **arrive** in the evening.

Last year we went to the beach ....
....
....
....
....
....
....
....
....

3 **Write negative sentences using the Past simple.**

1 we / not see / any sharks
  We didn't see any sharks.
2 he / not eat / the ice cream
  ....
3 there / not be / any boats
  ....
4 they / not play / beach volleyball
  ....
5 the children / not make / sandcastles
  ....

4 **Correct the sentences.**

1 Their parents got up early. (late)
  Their parents didn't get up early.
  They got up late.
2 Paul saw a dolphin. (big fish)
  ....
3 I swam in the swimming pool. (ocean)
  ....
4 Martha rode a pony. (horse)
  ....
5 The family had fish for dinner. (pizza)
  ....

• Past simple: questions

5 **Mark the correct questions.**

1 a Did you stay in Los Angeles?   ☑
  b Did you stayed in Los Angeles?   ☐
2 a Visited they the zoo?   ☐
  b Did they visit the zoo?   ☐
3 a Did he goes to Hollywood?   ☐
  b Did he go to Hollywood?   ☐
4 a Did she ate a hamburger?   ☐
  b Did she eat a hamburger?   ☐
5 a What did we see in the aquarium?   ☐
  b What saw we in the aquarium?   ☐

6 **Write questions to ask Dan about his vacation. Then look at the picture and write his answers.**

Eiffel Tower

TRAIN TICKET
TRAIN TICKET
TRAIN TICKET
TRAIN TICKET
Destination: PARIS
Date: 17 August

1 where / go
  Where did you go on vacation?
  I went to Paris.
2 how / travel
  ....
  ....
3 when / arrive
  ....
  ....
4 who / go with
  ....
  ....

Grammar Reference

• Be going to

Affirmative

I	'm (am) going to	start a blog tomorrow.
He/She/It	's (is) going to	start a blog tomorrow.
You/We/They	're (are) going to	start a blog tomorrow.

Negative

I	'm not (am not) going to	buy an e-book.
He/She/It	isn't (is not) going to	buy an e-book.
You/We/They	're not (are not) going to	buy an e-book.

Questions and short answers

Am I going to have broadband?	Yes, I am. / No, I'm not.
Is he/she/it going to have broadband?	Yes, he/she/it is. No, he/she/it isn't.
Are you/we/they going to have broadband?	Yes, you/we/they are. No, you/we/they aren't.

Wh questions

What are you going to do tomorrow?

Time expressions

tomorrow	next week	next month
next year	soon	at two o'clock

Use

- We use *be going to* to talk about plans and intentions for the future.
  She's going to take a flash drive to school.

Form

- To form the affirmative, we use the verb *to be* (**am**, **is** or **are**) + **going to** + main verb.
  I'm going to write an email this evening.

- To form the negative, we add *not* after *am, is* or *are*.
  We aren't going to watch TV. (= are not)

- The word order changes in questions:
  am/is/are + subject + ***going to*** + main verb.
  Is he going to buy a netbook tomorrow?

- In short answers, we do not repeat the main verb.
  A *Are you going to ask about broadband?*
  B *No, I'm not.*

• Present continuous for future arrangements

Affirmative

I	'm (am) having	a party tonight.
He/She/It	's (is) having	a party tonight.
You/We/They	're (are) having	a party tonight.

Negative

I	'm not (am not) flying	to the US next week.
He/She/It	isn't (is not) flying	to the US next week.
You/We/They	're not (are not) flying	to the US next week.

Questions and short answers

Am I staying at your house tomorrow?	Yes, I am. / No, I'm not.
Is he/she/it staying at your house tomorrow?	Yes, he/she/it is. No, he/she/it isn't.
Are you/we/they staying at your house tomorrow?	Yes, you/we/they are. No, you/we/they aren't.

Wh questions

Where are you going on Tuesday?

Time expressions

at nine o'clock	tomorrow	tomorrow evening
on Thursday	this afternoon	next weekend

Use

- We use the Present continuous to talk about future arrangements.
  I'm playing in a basketball game at three.

Grammar practice • Be going to

1 Write what each person is going to do. Use these phrases.

> charge his cell phone   play computer games
> read my e-book   send a text message
> ~~use a search engine~~

1 He*'s going to use a search engine.*
2 They ....
3 I ....
4 He ....
5 She ....

2 Complete the text with the correct form of *be going to*.

This Saturday, Paul, Ted and Josh [1] *are going to play* (play) with their band in the town square. Their friend, Becky, [2] .... (sing). The concert [3] .... (not start) until 9 p.m. There [4] .... (not be) any food, but there [5] .... (be) a lot of drinks for sale. All their friends [6] .... (go). Ted's dad [7] .... (make) a video, and they [8] .... (put) it on the Internet.

3 Read the answers and write questions.

> bank   ~~movie theater~~   post office
> supermarket   train station

1 *Are they going to go to the movie theater?*
   Yes. They're going to see a movie.
2 .... ?
   Yes. She's going to get some money.
3 .... ?
   Yes. I'm going to send some letters.
4 .... ?
   Yes. He's going to take the train to Boston.
5 .... ?
   Yes. They're going to buy some food.

• Present continuous for future arrangements

4 Mark the sentences about the future.

1 I'm flying to Greece tomorrow. ☑
2 At the moment, they're playing baseball in the park. ☐
3 Are you going to the dentist next week? ☐
4 The train's leaving this afternoon at four thirty. ☐
5 She's wearing a red dress and brown sandals today. ☐
6 Is he studying in his room? ☐

5 Complete the sentences with the Present continuous of the underlined verbs.

1 We <u>don't go skiing</u> in the spring. We *aren't going skiing* next month.
2 The planes <u>fly</u> to the US every day. The planes .... to the US tonight.
3 They <u>watch</u> TV in the evenings. They .... TV after dinner.
4 He <u>doesn't play</u> any sports. He .... soccer tomorrow.
5 I often <u>meet</u> my friends in the park. I .... them in the park after school.
6 She <u>stays</u> with her grandma every summer. She .... with her grandma next July.

6 Complete the questions.

1 Who *are you seeing* tomorrow?
   I'm seeing Dr. White.
2 Where .... on the weekend?
   He's going to San Francisco.
3 When .... ?
   They're coming back on Thursday.
4 What .... to the party on Friday?
   She's wearing her new green dress.
5 .... tonight?
   Yes. We're watching *Friends* on NBC.
6 What exams .... tomorrow?
   They're taking their Spanish and history exams.

Vocabulary 5

Out and About!

Unit vocabulary

1 Translate the words.

Activities

bowling ....

climbing ....

dancing ....

gymnastics ....

hiking ....

horseback riding

....

ice skating ....

kayaking ....

mountain biking

....

painting ....

playing an instrument

....

rollerblading ....

singing ....

surfing ....

2 Translate the words.

Seasons

spring ....

summer ....

autumn/fall ....

winter ....

Weather

cloudy ....

cold ....

foggy ....

hot ....

raining ....

snowing ....

sunny ....

warm ....

windy ....

Vocabulary extension

3 Match the photos to the words in the box. Use your dictionary if necessary. Write the words in English and in your language.

| flood | ice | lightning | rainbow | ~~storm~~ |

1 ..... *storm* ....

2 ....

3 ....

4 ....

5 ....
....

Vocabulary

Delicious!

Unit vocabulary

1 Translate the words.

Food and drinks

banana ....
bread ....
broccoli ....
cheese ....
chicken ....
eggs ....
ham ....
juice ....
pasta ....
rice ....
salmon ....
sausage ....
shrimp ....
tea ....
tomatoes ....
tuna ....
water ....
yogurt ....

2 Translate the words.

Adjectives

clean ....
cold ....
delicious ....
dirty ....
disgusting ....
horrible ....
hot ....
large ....
noisy ....
quiet ....
small ....
wonderful ....

Vocabulary extension

3 Match the photos to the words in the box. Use your dictionary if necessary. Write the words in English and in your language.

| carrots | cauliflower | cherries | ~~peaches~~ | peas |

1 ...*peaches*... .... 2 ....

3 .... 4 ....

5 ....
....

Vocabulary

Modern History

1 Translate the words.

Ordinal numbers and years

first ....
second ....
third ....
fourth ....
fifth ....
twentieth ....
twenty-second ....
thirty-first ....
nineteen twelve

....
nineteen twenty-two

....
nineteen forty-two

....
two thousand

....
two thousand four

....
two thousand eleven

....

2 Translate the words.

Regular verbs

answer ....
ask ....
call ....
close ....
invent ....
like ....
listen ....
stop ....
study ....
talk ....
travel ....
work ....

Vocabulary extension

3 Match the photos to the words in the box. Use your dictionary if necessary. Write the words in English and in your language.

| cook   do the dishes   help   open   sweep |

1 ....cook.......... .... 2 ....

3 .... 4 ....

5 ....
....

Vocabulary 8

Travel

1 Translate the words.

Means of transportation

bike ....
boat ....
bus ....
canoe ....
car ....
helicopter ....
motorcycle ....
plane ....
scooter ....
subway ....
train ....
truck ....
van ....
drive ....
fly ....
ride ....
sail ....
take ....

2 Translate the words.

Clothes

boots ....
coat ....
dress ....
hat ....
jeans ....
pajamas ....
pants ....
sandals ....
scarf ....
shorts ....
skirt ....
sneakers ....
sweater ....

Vocabulary extension

3 Match the photos to the words in the box. Use your dictionary if necessary. Write the words in English and in your language.

~~belt~~   gloves   jacket   slippers   socks

1 .... *belt* ....

2 ....

3 ....

4 ....

5 ....
....

Vocabulary

Technology Time

Unit vocabulary

1 Translate the words.

Technology
blog ....
broadband ....
digital radio ....
e-reader ....
flash drive ....
IM (instant messaging)
....
interactive whiteboard
....
netbook ....
screen ....
smart phone ....
social networking site
....
Wi-Fi ....

2 Translate the phrases.

Technology phrases
charge your cell phone
....
chat online ....
download movies
....
download music
....
download videos
....
go online ....
send an email ....
send a text ....
use a search engine
....
use the Internet ....
use Wi-Fi ....
write a blog ....

Vocabulary extension

3 Match the photos to the words in the box. Use your dictionary if necessary. Write the words in English and in your language.

| document | keyboard | ~~mouse~~ | mouse pad | printer |

1 ......*mouse*...... .... **2** ....

3 .... **4** ....

5 ....
....

Speaking and Listening

Expressing surprise

• Speaking

1 Match the statements (1–5) to the responses
51 (a–e). Then listen and check.

wild deer

1 This is a beautiful place. It's very quiet.   *e*
2 The mail carrier's here. There's a letter for you.
3 That store sells cheap posters.
4 I got Taylor Swift's autograph!
5 We have tickets for *American Idol*!

a Oh really? Great! I want a new poster
  for my room.
b Wow! How cool! When is it?
c Really? Who's it from?
d How amazing! Can you get it for me, too?
e Look! There are some deer over there.

2 Read the conversation and choose the
52 correct options. Then listen and check.

Dad	¹ We're here! / See you later.
Harry	Are we staying in this room?
Dad	Yes, we are.
Harry	² *Yuck!* / *Wow!* It's awesome. The beds are big.
Lizzie	And there's a computer and a TV.
Harry	We can see the town square from our window.
Lizzie	³ *I don't know.* / *Look!* There's a purple statue.
Harry	That isn't a real ⁴ *statue* / *purple*. It's a man on a box!
Lizzie	⁵ *Really?* / *Amazing?* It looks real.
Harry	I know. It's so ⁶ *cool* / *favorite*.
Lizzie	Dad, can we go and take a photo of him?
Dad	OK, but come back quickly.

• Listening

3 Listen to the conversation. Are the statements
53 true (T) or false (F)?

1 Brenda is Richard's aunt.   *T*
2 Her visit is a surprise.
3 She gives Richard a bike.
4 She stays for dinner.
5 Richard goes to the studio with Brenda.

4 Listen again. Answer the questions.
53
1 Who does Richard tell that Brenda's here?
  He tells his mom and dad.
2 Why does Brenda give Richard a present?
  ....
3 What does Brenda give him?
  ....
4 When is Brenda's interview?
  ....
5 Where is the interview?
  ....

Speaking and Listening

Ordering food

• Speaking

1 Match the questions (1–5) to the answers (a–e).
54 Then listen and check.

1 Can we sit here, please?   *d*
2 Are you ready to order?
3 Would you like some garlic bread?
4 Would you like anything to drink?
5 How is your food?

a No, thank you.
b It's delicious.
c Yes, we are.
d Yes, of course. Here's the menu.
e Yes. I'd like a glass of water, please.

2 Complete the conversation with these words.
55 Then listen and check.

anything	glass	I'll	like
OK	ready	~~table~~	Would

Boy   Let's sit at this ¹ *table*.
Dad   Yes. It's better than the table
            next to the door.
Waiter Are you ² .... to order?
Boy   I am. I'd like an egg sandwich and
            a strawberry smoothie, please.
Dad   And ³ .... have a chicken
            sandwich with mayonnaise, please.
Waiter Would you like ⁴ .... to drink?
Dad   Can I have a ⁵ .... of orange
            juice, please?
Waiter Yes, of course. ⁶ .... you like
            some chips with your sandwiches?
Dad   No. I'm ⁷ .... , thanks.
Boy   I'd ⁸ .... some chips, please.

• Listening

3 Listen to the conversation. Choose
56 the correct options.

1 They sit next to the *door / (window.)*
2 The waiter gives them *some water / the menus*.
3 Olivia would like *pasta / chicken* with
   tomato sauce.
4 Two people drink *orange / apple* juice.
5 They are in a *restaurant / café*.

4 Listen again. Complete the order.
56

Food	Drinks
• Customer 1	
.... with tomato sauce	orange juice
• Customer 2	
.... and broccoli	....
• Customer 3	
ham and cheese	apple juice

Speaking and Listening

Talking about the past

• Speaking

1 Complete the sentences with these time words
57 and phrases. Then listen and check.

minutes ago	morning	~~night~~
seven years	the 1970s	yesterday

1 **A** Where were they last *night*?
  B They were at home.
2 **A** Was there any homework .... ?
  B No, there wasn't.
3 He was late to school this ....
4 The teacher was in the classroom
  five ....
5 I like clothes from ....
6 He went to that school for ....

2 Complete the conversation with these words
58 and phrases. Then listen and check.

ago	didn't	~~for~~	last
twenty	yesterday	1980s	

Dad Look! That's our old house. We lived
there ¹ *for* five years.
Clara I don't remember it.
Dad You ² .... live there. I lived
there in the ³ .... when I was
a child.
Clara I didn't know you were from Atlanta.
Dad Yes, Grandma and Grandpa moved to
San Diego about ⁴ .... years
⁵ ....
Clara I like their new house. Can we visit them
this weekend?
Dad Sure. Grandma called me ⁶ ....
Grandpa painted the living room orange
⁷ .... week. I want to see it!
Clara Me too! It sounds amazing!

• Listening

3 Listen to the conversation. Are the statements
59 true (T) or false (F)?

1 Donna Martin is an actor.   T
2 She arrived in Canada last month.   .....
3 This is her first visit.   .....
4 Her new movie is called *Generation Rox*.   .....
5 The movie is about three girls.   .....
6 Donna thinks the movie is very funny.   .....

4 Listen again. Answer the questions.
59
1 Where does Donna come from?
  She's from the US.
2 When was she in Canada?
  ....
3 When were the girls in the movie in New York?
  ....
4 How long were the girls in New York?
  ....
5 What music does Donna like?
  ....

Speaking and Listening

Talking on the phone

• Speaking

(1) **Complete the conversations with the correct**
60 **phrase. Then listen and check.**

> Is Justin there, please?   Just a minute.
> ~~This is her mom.~~   Who's this?

1

Bonnie's mom	Hello.
Ira	Hello. Is this Bonnie?
Bonnie's mom	No, it isn't. *This is her mom.*

2

Denzil	Hello.
Natalie	Hello. Is Frank there?
Denzil	Yes, he is. ....
Natalie	It's Natalie.

3

Cathy	Hello. This is Cathy.
Justin's dad	Hi, Cathy.
Cathy	....
Justin's dad	No, I'm sorry. Justin isn't here at the moment.

4

Charlie	Hello. This is Charlie. Can I speak to Anita, please?
Cameron	.... – Anita, Charlie's on the phone for you!

(2) **Read the conversation and choose the correct**
61 **options. Then listen and check.**

Brad's dad	Hello.
Connie	¹ *Hold on* / (*Hello*) is this Brad?
Brad's dad	No, it isn't. ² *This is* / *I am* his dad.
Connie	Oh. Hi, Mr. Jones. Can I ³ *speak* / *have* to Brad, please?
Brad's dad	Yes, of course. ⁴ *See* / *Here* he is.
Connie	Hi, Brad. It's me, Connie.
Brad	Hello, Connie. How are you?
Connie	I'm fine, ⁵ *please* / *thanks*. Do you have Jordan's cell phone number?
Brad	Yes, ⁶ *only* / *just* a minute. It's 377 950-3729.
Connie	That's great. Thanks very much. Bye!
Brad	See you ⁷ *later* / *minute*.

• Listening

(3) **Listen to the telephone conversation. These**
62 **sentences are useful for talking on the phone.**
Mark the sentences you hear.

1 Joel here.	☐
Joel speaking.	☑
2 Can I speak to Eve, please?	☐
Is Eve there, please?	☐
3 Who's speaking, please?	☐
Who is it, please?	☐
4 Just a minute.	☐
Hold on.	☐
5 Can you speak up, please?	☐
Can you talk louder, please?	☐

(4) **Listen again. Answer the questions.**
62

1 What club does Rob ask about?
He asks about the Wildlife Club.

2 Did Eve go to the club yesterday?
....

3 Where is the trip to?
....

4 What date is the trip?
....

5 Can Rob go on the trip?
....

Speaking and Listening

Asking for information

• Speaking

1 Match the questions (1–5) to the answers (a–e).
63 Then listen and check.

1 What happened last night?   *d*
2 What are you going to do?
3 I downloaded that new movie yesterday.
4 Can you tell us more about your blog?
5 What is she planning for next year?

a I'm going to send an email to the principal.
b Tell me about it.
c She's going to study computer science.
d I dropped my phone, and it doesn't work now.
e I write about our band and all our concerts.

2 Complete the conversation with these words.
64 Then listen and check.

bank	car		going	happened
more	~~newspaper~~		saw	Tell

Bank Robbery Buffalo

Will Wow! Look at this ¹ *newspaper* article.
It's about a bank robbery here in Buffalo.
Ross Oh, yes!
Will Well, I ² .... the robbers.
Ross Really? ³ .... me about it.
Will Last Saturday morning I was downtown,
outside the ⁴ .... Suddenly two
men got out of a ⁵ ....
Ross What ⁶ .... next? Tell me
⁷ ....
Will They ran into the bank. I'm sure they were
the robbers. I saw them very clearly.
Ross What are you ⁸ .... to do?
Will I'm going to tell the police what I saw.

• Listening

3 Listen to the conversation. Are the statements
65 true (T) or false (F)?

1 Simon fell off his bike.   *T*
2 A boy ran in front of the bike.   .....
3 The dog was hurt.   .....
4 Simon is going to ride his bike
in the park after dinner.   .....
5 There's a good movie on TV in the evening. .....

4 Listen again. Answer the questions.
65
1 Where were Paul and Simon?
They were in the park.
2 Was it Paul's dog?
....
3 Did Simon hit the dog?
....
4 Is Simon's leg clean?
....
5 What is Simon going to do this evening?
....

Pronunciation

Consonants

Symbol	Example	Your examples
/p/	park	
/b/	big	
/t/	talk	
/d/	dog	
/k/	car	
/g/	good	
/tʃ/	chair	
/dʒ/	jump	
/f/	fly	
/v/	video	
/θ/	three	
/ð/	they	
/s/	swim	
/z/	zoo	
/ʃ/	shop	
/ʒ/	television	
/h/	hot	
/m/	meet	
/n/	new	
/ŋ/	sing	
/l/	laptop	
/r/	room	
/j/	yellow	
/w/	watch	

Vowels

Symbol	Example	Your examples
/ɪ/	insect	
/ɛ/	leg	
/æ/	ham	
/ɑ/	box	
/ʌ/	fun	
/ʊ/	put	
/i/	eat	
/eɪ/	sail	
/aɪ/	my	
/ɔɪ/	boy	
/u/	boot	
/oʊ/	phone	
/aʊ/	now	
/ɪr/	hear	
/ɛr/	hair	
/ɑr/	arm	
/ɔ/	dog	
/ʊr/	tour	
/ɔr/	door	
/ə/	among	
/ɚ/	shirt	

Pronunciation practice

Unit 1 • Short forms

1 **Listen and repeat.**
66
1 I do not have   I don't have
2 He does not have   He doesn't have
3 They do not have   They don't have
4 She does not have   She doesn't have

2 **Listen. Mark the sentence you hear.**
67
1 a We do not have the camera. ☐
  b We don't have the camera. ☐
2 a The dog does not have the ball. ☐
  b The dog doesn't have the ball. ☐
3 a You do not have your wallet. ☐
  b You don't have your wallet. ☐
4 a He does not have a watch. ☐
  b He doesn't have a watch. ☐

3 **Listen and repeat.**
68
1 She doesn't have a ruler.
2 I don't have an eraser.
3 He doesn't have a pen.
4 You don't have a game console.

Unit 2 • Silent letters

1 **Listen and repeat.**
69
1 The snake can't walk, but it can swim.
2 I know your sister.
3 Talk to the man in the bank.
4 It can run and climb trees.
5 The guitar's on the table.

2 **Which words from Exercise 1 have a silent letter? Write the words.**
1 ....
2 ....
3 ....
4 ....
5 ....

3 **Listen and check.**
70

Unit 3 • -s endings

1 **Listen and repeat.**
71
1 likes   /s/   She likes me.
2 plays   /z/   He plays in the backyard.
3 watches   /ɪz/   The cat watches the birds.

2 **Listen and complete the table with these verbs.**
72

| dances | flies | jumps |
| runs | walks | washes |

/s/	/z/	/ɪz/
....	....	....
....	....	....

3 **Listen and check.**
73

Unit 4 • Contrastive stress

1 **Listen and repeat.**
74
1 **A** I can't swim.
  B No, but you can skate. I can't.
2 **A** Jess likes playing soccer.
  B Really? I don't. I like playing basketball.
3 Peter likes watching movies. But Derek likes playing computer games.
4 I have a new watch.
5 **A** There's a cat in the backyard.
  B No, there isn't. That's our dog!

2 **Listen again. Circle the stressed words in Exercise 1.**
74

3 **Listen and check.**
75

Unit 5 • -ing endings

1 **Listen and repeat.**
76
1 eat   eating   3 climb   climbing
2 dance   dancing

2 **Listen. Circle the word you hear.**
77
1 skate   skating   4 sing   singing
2 rainy   raining   5 clean   cleaning
3 study   studying   6 start   starting

3 Listen and repeat.

78
1 He's going to school.
2 We're running.
3 She's having lunch.
4 They're swimming.
5 I'm playing a computer game.

Unit 6 • Word stress

1 Listen and repeat.

79

• •	• • •
chicken	po<u>ta</u>to

2 Listen and choose the word with the correct stress.

80

• • 1 <u>yo</u>gurt	• • yo<u>gurt</u>
• • 2 <u>carr</u>ot	• • car<u>rot</u>
• • • 3 bro<u>cco</u>li	• • • broccoli
• • 4 <u>dairy</u>	• • dairy
• • 5 <u>wa</u>ter	• • water
• • • 6 to<u>ma</u>to	• • • to<u>ma</u>to
• • 7 <u>tu</u>na	• • tu<u>na</u>
• • • 8 ba<u>na</u>na	• • • ba<u>na</u>na
• • 9 <u>sal</u>mon	• • sal<u>mon</u>
• • 10 pas<u>ta</u>	• • pasta

3 Listen and check.

81

Unit 7 • -ed endings

1 Listen and repeat.

82
1 listened   /d/   We <u>listened</u> to the teacher.
2 invented   /ɪd/   He <u>invented</u> the radio.
3 talked   /t/   She <u>talked</u> to her friend.

2 Listen and complete the table with these words.

83

called	liked	opened
started	wanted	watched

/d/	/ɪd/	/t/
....	....	....
....	....	....

3 Listen and check.

84

Unit 8 • Sounding polite

1 Listen to two versions of the same phone conversation. Which sounds more polite?

85

Debbie's sister   Hello.
Jake   Hi. This is Jake. Is this Debbie?
Debbie's sister   No, it's her sister. Do you want to talk to her?
Jake   Yes. Is she there?
Debbie's sister   Yes, she is. Just a minute.

2 Listen. Decide which pronunciation is polite (P) and which is not polite (NP).

86
1 a Can I speak to Dave, please?
   b Can I speak to Dave, please?
2 a Who's speaking, please?
   b Who's speaking, please?
3 a This is Liam's dad.
   b This is Liam's dad.

3 Listen and repeat.

87

Unit 9 • Weak form of *to*

1 Listen and repeat.

88
1 It's going to snow.
2 They aren't going to go on vacation.
3 Is he going to buy the DVD?

2 Listen and mark the sentences with the weak form of *to*.

89

1 ☐	3 ☐	5 ☐
2 ☐	4 ☐	6 ☐

3 Listen and check.

90

Irregular Verb List

Verb	Past Simple	Past Particple
be	was/were	been
become	became	become
begin	began	begun
break	broke	broken
bring	brought	brought
build	built	built
buy	bought	bought
can	could	been able
catch	caught	caught
choose	chose	chosen
come	came	come
cost	cost	cost
cut	cut	cut
do	did	done
drink	drank	drunk
drive	drove	driven
eat	ate	eaten
feel	felt	felt
fight	fought	fought
find	found	found
fly	flew	flown
forget	forgot	forgotten
get	got	gotten
give	gave	given
go	went	gone/been
have	had	had
hear	heard	heard
hold	held	held
keep	kept	kept

Verb	Past Simple	Past Particple
know	knew	known
leave	left	left
lose	lost	lost
make	made	made
mean	meant	meant
meet	met	met
pay	paid	paid
put	put	put
read /rid/	read /rɛd/	read /rɛd/
run	ran	run
say	said	said
see	saw	seen
sell	sold	sold
send	sent	sent
sing	sang	sung
sit	sat	sat
sleep	slept	slept
speak	spoke	spoken
swim	swam	swum
take	took	taken
teach	taught	taught
tell	told	told
think	thought	thought
throw	threw	thrown
understand	understood	understood
wake	woke	woken
wear	wore	worn
win	won	won
write	wrote	written

My Assessment Profile   Unit

1 **What can I do? Mark (✓) the options in the table.**

⏪ = I need to study this again.   ⏸ = I'm not sure about this.   ▶ = I'm happy with this.   ⏩ = I do this very well.

		⏪	⏸	▶	⏩
Vocabulary (pages 4 and 7)	• I can describe different freetime activities. • I can talk about the weather and the seasons.				
Reading (pages 5 and 10)	• I can read a magazine article about a stuntman's day and understand some poems about the weather.				
Grammar (pages 6 and 9)	• I can use the Present continuous to talk about things that are happening now. • I can decide when to use the Present continuous and when to use the Present simple.				
Pronunciation (page 6)	• I can pronounce the Present continuous ending -ing.				
Speaking (pages 8 and 9)	• I can express surprise in different situations.				
Listening (page 10)	• I can understand people describing their preferences.				
Writing (page 11)	• I can write a blog entry about an exchange trip.				

2 **What new words and expressions can I remember?**

words ....

expressions ....

3 **How can I practice other new words and expressions?**

record them on my MP3 player ☐   write them in a notebook ☐

practice them with a friend ☐   translate them into my language ☐

4 **What English have I learned outside class?**

	words	expressions
on the radio		
in songs		
in movies		
on the Internet		
on TV		
with friends		

My Assessment Profile Unit

1 What can I do? Mark (✓) the options in the table.

⏮ = I need to study this again. ⏸ = I'm not sure about this. ▶ = I'm happy with this. ⏭ = I do this very well.

		⏮	⏸	▶	⏭
Vocabulary (pages 14 and 17)	• I can talk about different types of food and drinks, and food categories. • I can use contrasting adjectives.				
Reading (pages 15 and 20)	• I can read a magazine article about food and understand a newspaper feature about special restaurants.				
Grammar (pages 16 and 19)	• I can use countable and uncountable nouns and *(how) many/ (how) much/a lot of.* • I can make comparisons using short or long adjectives.				
Pronunciation (page 16)	• I can hear the stress in different words for food and drinks.				
Speaking (pages 18 and 19)	• I can order food.				
Listening (page 20)	• I can understand people giving different information about national dishes.				
Writing (page 21)	• I can use the sequence words *first, then* and *finally.* • I can write instructions for a recipe.				

2 What new words and expressions can I remember?

words ....

expressions ....

3 How can I practice other new words and expressions?

record them on my MP3 player ☐ write them in a notebook ☐

practice them with a friend ☐ translate them into my language ☐

4 What English have I learned outside class?

	words	expressions
on the radio		
in songs		
in movies		
on the Internet		
on TV		
with friends		

My Assessment Profile Unit 7

1 What can I do? Mark (✓) the options in the table.

⏪ = I need to study this again. ⏸ = I'm not sure about this. ▶ = I'm happy with this. ⏩ = I do this very well.

		⏪	⏸	▶	⏩
Vocabulary (pages 28 and 31)	• I can use and talk about ordinal numbers, years and dates. • I can use regular verbs.				
Reading (pages 29 and 34)	• I can read the text of a school project about the 1960s and understand a brochure for a museum exhibition about modern culture.				
Grammar (pages 30 and 33)	• I can use the Past simple of *to be* and *there was/there were.* • I can make statements using Past simple regular verbs.				
Pronunciation (page 31)	• I can hear the difference between the Past simple *-ed* endings /d/, /t/ and /ɪd/.				
Speaking (pages 32 and 33)	• I can use expressions to talk about the past.				
Listening (page 34)	• I can understand people describing what they do in a museum.				
Writing (page 35)	• I can use periods, commas, question marks and exclamation points. • I can write an essay about childhood.				

2 What new words and expressions can I remember?

words ....

expressions ....

3 How can I practice other new words and expressions?

record them on my MP3 player ☐
practice them with a friend ☐
write them in a notebook ☐
translate them into my language ☐

4 What English have I learned outside class?

	words	expressions
on the radio		
in songs		
in movies		
on the Internet		
on TV		
with friends		

My Assessment Profile   Unit

1 **What can I do? Mark (✓) the options in the table.**

⏮ = I need to study this again.   ⏸ = I'm not sure about this.   ▶ = I'm happy with this.   ⏭ = I do this very well.

		⏮	⏸	▶	⏭
Vocabulary (pages 38 and 41)	• I can talk about different means of transportation and use transportation verbs. • I can talk about clothes.				
Reading (pages 39 and 44)	• I can read an extract from a novel about a journey around the world and understand information from a textbook about a boy living in West Africa.				
Grammar (pages 40 and 43)	• I can make statements using Past simple irregular verbs. • I can ask questions using the Past simple.				
Pronunciation (page 43)	• I can sound polite.				
Speaking (pages 42 and 43)	• I can use the correct phrases for talking on the phone.				
Listening (page 44)	• I can understand an informal conversation.				
Writing (page 45)	• I can use paragraphs correctly in a text. • I can write a travel diary.				

2 **What new words and expressions can I remember?**

words ....

expressions ....

3 **How can I practice other new words and expressions?**

record them on my MP3 player ☐   write them in a notebook ☐
practice them with a friend ☐   translate them into my language ☐

4 **What English have I learned outside class?**

	words	expressions
on the radio		
in songs		
in movies		
on the Internet		
on TV		
with friends		

My Assessment Profile Unit

1 What can I do? Mark (✓) the options in the table.

⏪ = I need to study this again. ⏸ = I'm not sure about this. ▶ = I'm happy with this. ⏩ = I do this very well.

		⏪	⏸	▶	⏩
Vocabulary (pages 48 and 51)	• I can talk about different types of technology. • I can use technology phrases.				
Reading (pages 49 and 54)	• I can understand a magazine article about e-books and read chatroom entries about a technology-free week at school.				
Grammar (pages 50 and 53)	• I can use *be going to* to talk about future plans and intentions. • I can use the Present continuous to talk about future arrangements.				
Pronunciation (page 50)	• I can pronounce the weak form of *to* in *going to*.				
Speaking (pages 52 and 53)	• I can use phrases to ask for information.				
Listening (page 54)	• I can understand people talking about their plans.				
Writing (page 55)	• I can check my writing for mistakes. • I can write a story.				

2 What new words and expressions can I remember?

words ....

expressions ....

3 How can I practice other new words and expressions?

record them on my MP3 player ☐   write them in a notebook ☐

practice them with a friend ☐   translate them into my language ☐

4 What English have I learned outside class?

	words	expressions
on the radio		
in songs		
in movies		
on the Internet		
on TV		
with friends		

Notes

Notes

Notes

Notes

Notes

Pearson Education Limited

Edinburgh Gate

Harlow

Essex CM20 2JE

England

and Associated Companies throughout the world.

www.pearsonelt.com/moveit

© Pearson Education Limited 2015

The right of Carolyn Barraclough, Katherine Stannett and Charlotte Covill to be identified as the authors of this work has been asserted by them in accordance with the Copyright, Designs and Patents Act, 1988.

First published 2015

Tenth impression 2020

Set in 10.5/12.5pt LTC Helvetica Neue Light

ISBN: 978-1-2921-0132-3

Acknowledgements

We are grateful to the following for permission to reproduce copyright material:

Poetry on page 10 'Weather' from *101 Science Poems & Songs for Young Learners* by Meish Goldish. Scholastic Inc./Teaching Resources. Copyright © 1996 by Meish Goldish. Reprinted by permission.

Photo Acknowledgements

The publisher would like to thank the following for their kind permission to reproduce their photographs:

(Key: b-bottom; c-centre; l-left; r-right; t-top)

Students' Book:

123RF.com: Tono Balaguer 67t, Songquan Deng 69bc; akg-images Ltd: 34 (d); Alamy Images: Design Pics Inc. 8bl, Jonathan Goldberg 4/8, History Archives 68br, David L. Moore 4/7, Photos 12 55; Bridgeman Art Library Ltd: National Geographic Image Collection 28/1; Corbis: Bettmann 28/8, Edith Held 4/13, I Love Images 4/14, Image Source 4/10, Tim Pannell 11, Radius Images 4/12, Tom Stewart 4/4, Tiziana and Gianni Baldizzone 44; Fotolia.com: alpegor 67bc (left), bagpereira 48/9, Marilyn Barbone 4/9, chrisberic 4/3, cphoto 48/5, D.aniel 67bc (right), dfarocunha 67bl, Richard Griffin 41tr, Hemeroskopion 49b, highwaystarz 69tc, jirkacafa 48/1, Olga Kovalenko 48/12, Monkey Business 69t, pio3 67br, rgbdigital. co.uk 48/3, robynmac 29cr, RTimages 48/8, sarsmis 69b, Nikolai Sorokin 48/2, Stocksnapper 16, Suteracher 10br, WuTtY 48/11; Getty Images: 20l, 28/2, 28/6, 28/7, AFP 28/4, Gerard Fritz 5tr, Bruce Gardner 5br, Jean-Marc Giboux 34 (a), Jetta Productions 51br, Jupiter 10l, NY Daily News 28/5, Popperfoto 29tr, SSPL 29b, Universal Images Group 68tr, Joseph Wright of Derby 68tl; Guardian News and Media Ltd: Xan Rice 47t; iStockphoto: espion 10tr, Rich Legg 4/5, Stas Perov 5bl; Photo Courtesy of James Koper: 23r; Mary Evans Picture Library: Interfoto Agentur 29cl, Marx Memorial Library 28/3; Pacific Environment Architects: 20c; Pearson Education Ltd: Jon Barlow 40l, 40r, Gareth Boden 4/11; Pearson Education Ltd: Jon Barlow 8, 14, 15, 18, 32, 42l, 42r, 52, 62, 63, 64, 65l, 65r, 66; Photofusion Picture Library: David Tothill 57; Photoshot Holdings Limited: Retna 35r; Rex Features: Andre Csillag 34 (c), dinnerinthesky.com / Solent 20r, Tim Rooke 47b; Shutterstock.com: Bloomua 49t,

Stephen Bonk 4/1, Warren Goldswain 5tl, Sergiy Zavgorodny 4/2, 4/6; Amy Singh: 23l; The Kobal Collection: 4 Kids Entertainment 35l, MGM 68bl, Paramount 34 (b), Universal 34 (e), 34 (f); TopFoto: 29tl

Workbook:

123RF.com: Barbara Helgason 83tr, Dzianis Miraniuk 98tr; Alamy Images: Angela Hampton Picture Library 104cl, Ffotocymru 81bl, Rafael Angel Irusta Machin 136tr, Bob Paroue-SC 106; Comstock Images: 129tr; Corbis: Atlantide Phototravel / Massimo Borchi 133cl, Comet / Randy Faris 125, Corbis Outline / Steve Ellison 88, HO / Reuters 98tc, Imagesource 79tr, Norgues-Orban / Sygma 92bl, Xinhua Press / Chen Kai 92tc; Digital Vision: Robert Harding World Imagery / Jim Reed 128tl; Fotolia.com: 142-146; Getty Images: GP / Ivan Gavan 98tl, Dave Hogan 78r, OJO Images / Robert Daly 135tr, Retrofile RF / George Marks 93cr, Alberto E. Rodriguez 78c, WireImage / Jim Spellman 78l; MedioImages: 105tr; MIXA Co., Ltd: 83br; NASA: 92tr; National Archives and Records Administration (NARA): 92tl; Pearson Education Ltd: Jon Barlow 134cr, Sophie Bluy 83bc, Ikat Design / Ann Cromack 102br, Jules Selmes 83bl, 93bl, 104c, 135cl, Studio 8 80tc; Reuters: Vincent Kessler 101tr; Rex Features: Sipa Press 92br; Science Photo Library Ltd: Ria Novosti 92bc; Shutterstock.com: Aispix by Imagesource 79bc, Ozerov Alexander 128cl, Alexgul 132tl, Anetapics 137tr, Blend 79bl, Creatista 133cr, Deklofenak 130cl, Hfng 79tc, Holbox 79tl, IKO 109cl, Lobur Alexey Ivanovich 131tl, Jhaz Photography 128cr, Karkas 131cr, Lori B.K. Mann 128b, Maridav 79br, Jiri Miklo 130tl, Robert Milek 132cl, Monkey Business Images 130tr, Olinchuk 131b, Olga Popova 131cl, pressureUA 109tl, PRILL Mediendesign und Fotografie 129b, Christina Richards 130b, Roberts.J 83cl, ronfromyork 128tr, Sagir 131tr, Santia 129cl, Shutswis 132tr, Artur Synenko 132cr, Pal Teravagimov 133tl, Vadico 83cr, Vanillaechoes 83tl, Vilax 109c, Valentyn Volkov 129tl, 129cr, Wavebreakmedia Ltd 130cr, Yurok 132b; The Independent: 101tl; The Kobal Collection: Universal 96bl; Zuma Press: Los Angeles Daily News / Michael Owen Baker 101cl

Cover images: Front: Alamy Images: Design Pics Inc.

All other images © Pearson Education

Every effort has been made to trace the copyright holders and we apologise in advance for any unintentional omissions. We would be pleased to insert the appropriate acknowledgement in any subsequent edition of this publication.

Special thanks to the following for their help during location photography:

Ascape Studios; Herts Young Mariners Base; Lullingstone Country Park; Pets Corner; Soprano, Sevenoaks; St. Matthew Academy; The Stag Community Arts Centre.

Illustrated by

Students' Book:

Alfonso Abad; Sonia Alins; Maxwell Dorsey; Paula Franco; Kate Rochester; Marcela Gómez Ruenes (A Corazón Abierto).

Workbook:

Alfonso Abad; Sonia Alins; Moreno Chiacchiera; Paula Franco; Nancy Ortega; Kate Rochester; Marcela Gómez Ruenes (A Corazón Abierto).

Printed and bound in Italy by L.E.G.O. S.p.A.